SHAPING THE CORPORATE IMAGE

Shaping the Corporate Image

AN ANALYTICAL GUIDE FOR EXECUTIVE DECISION MAKERS

Marion G. Sobol,
Gail E. Farrelly,
and Jessica S. Taper

Q

Quorum Books
NEW YORK • WESTPORT, CONNECTICUT • LONDON

Library of Congress Cataloging-in-Publication Data

Sobol, Marion Gross.
 Shaping the corporate image : an analytical guide for executive
decision makers / Marion G. Sobol, Gail E. Farrelly, and Jessica S.
Taper.
  p. cm.
 Includes bibliographical references and index.
 ISBN 0–89930–564–4 (alk. paper)
 1. Corporate image. I. Farrelly, Gail E. II. Taper, Jessica S.
III. Title.
HD59.2.S67 1992
659.2—dc20 91–38239

British Library Cataloguing in Publication Data is available.

Library of Congress Catalog Card Number: 91–38239
ISBN: 0–89930–564–4

First published in 1992

Quorum Books, One Madison Avenue, New York, NY 10010
An imprint of Greenwood Publishing Group, Inc.

Printed in the United States of America

The paper used in this book complies with the
Permanent Paper Standard issued by the National
Information Standards Organization (Z39.48–1984).

10 9 8 7 6 5 4 3 2 1

Copyright Acknowledgments

The authors and publisher gratefully acknowledge permission to use the following:

Anne S. Tsui, "A Role Set Analysis of Managerial Reputation," *Organizational Behavior & Human Decision Processes*. vol. 34 (1984).

Tables 2.1, 2.2, 4.2, 5.1, and 5.2. Data reprinted by permission of *Fortune* Magazine, ©1991 The Time Inc. Magazine Company. All rights reserved.

Debbie Galant "Gimmicks of the Year," *Institutional Investor*. (April 1990): 124–126.

Cutlip, Center, and Broom, *Effective Public Relations* 6/E, ©1985, 178–179. Reprinted by permission of Prentice-Hall, Inc. Englewood Cliffs, NJ, 07632.

Amanda Bennett, "How Business Measures Up," *Wall Street Journal*, November 12, 1990, B1.

Great Western Ad in *Wall Street Journal*, July18, 1990, B6.

To Harold, Rita, and Howard

Contents

Tables and Exhibits

TABLES

EXHIBITS

CHAPTER 1

Introduction

Most would agree that it is important for firms to have a good reputation, yet exactly what reputation means is open to question. *Webster's* provides several definitions of the word "reputation." It is interesting that the first definition is "The character commonly imputed to a person or thing; one's reputed as distinct from one's inherent or real character; as, honorable in spite of his *reputation*." Other definitions follow—repute, or public esteem; fame; celebrity; distinction; good name. But the first one is the most interesting, because it raises the possibility, maybe even the probability, that one can enjoy a good reputation without really deserving it. And this is the view of reputation that in general seems to dominate. Often when reputation is discussed, it is in terms of appearances. This raises the question of whether firms with good reputations are really "good," or whether they just *appear* to be good. Is it perception or reality that rules the market, or perhaps a little of each?

Financial theorists insist that, for the most part, markets are efficient (that is, that security prices fully reflect all of the information available in the marketplace). When regulators, academics, customers, and the general public plea for more disclosure, however, there are often strong protests from corporations. This causes some doubt about the true efficiency of the market and the quantity and quality of the information upon which market prices are based.

Thus, one is left to wonder: Do the firms with good reputations really deserve them? Would reputation rankings be different if there were more and better information available to financial analysts and the general public? What does it really mean to say that a firm has a good reputation? How does a firm both build and lose a good reputation?

Can a firm build its own reputation by slicing down others in the same industry? Shakespeare's Iago says, "He that filches from me my good name robs me of that which not enriches him, and makes me poor indeed." But Iago's statement does not seem to apply to corporate reputation. For a firm that sucessfully slices away a competitor's reputation can help itself, by increasing its own market share. By the same token, there is always the possibility that the one who slings the mud also gets dirty. Customers, not unlike voters in a political election, may react negatively to a corporation that constantly knocks its competitors.

This book is designed to consider the above issues, as well as numerous others. Due to recent happenings in financial markets, this seems like a good time to study reputation. Day by day, we are seeing fallout from numerous financial deals completed during the 1980s. The press is filled with reports of highly leveraged firms seeking to fend off bankruptcy. These are deals in which numbers alone, such as sales and earnings per share, predicted success (at least according to Wall Street analysts), but the predictions were just plain wrong. This seems to suggest that some qualitative factors accounted for the failure of these firms to achieve the level of success predicted. Reputation may be an important factor here, although it is a factor that is difficult to include in quantitative models. Even in acquisitions, an ownership switch may mean differences in customer perception of quality;

and perceptions, whether or not they are based in fact, rule the market. Employees finding themselves with a new boss, perhaps with poor reputation as an employer, may not be as motivated as they once were. And this lack of motivation may be expressed in the lower quality and quantity of goods and services produced ✳Reputation is an interesting topic because it blends finance, management, marketing, advertising, and public relations. The investor able to accurately assess reputation may have a great edge because a lot of complex happenings in the market may be explained by the concept of reputation. The consumer, too, would like to rely on reputation when buying an expensive product.

The topic of corporate reputation is an involved one, and it is wise to consider many different sources. Therefore, in discussing the topic in this book, we will cull research from many areas— *Fortune* surveys on corporate reputation, the academic literature, and numerous articles from the financial and popular press. The bibliography at the back of the book will allow interested readers to pursue specific issues that are of most interest to them.

✳Corporate reputation is a very important asset for a firm. Corporate image is particularly valuable in terms of ability to raise debt and equity capital. In addition, in the determination of product sales, corporate reputation is very helpful. For example, in the microcomputer market, even though IBM did not have the most innovative or cheapest personal computer offering in the market, it initially made rapid inroads into the market largely because of company reputation (Verity 1984).

Firms gain credibility for financial statements by "renting" the reputations of outside auditors. Many firms retain "big six" accounting firms not only to review their financial statements, but also to lend their name to the credibility of the company's statements (Kreps and Wilson 1982). In the service sector, which is rapidly increasing in economic importance, evaluation of potential service quality is vague and partial. Thus, lawyers, doctors, investment brokers, insurance companies, and accountants rely on outlets in high-rent districts, well-furnished offices, contributions to social causes, or sponsorship of athletic events to signal quality for their services and build their image (Milgrom and Roberts 1982).

Conversely, firms that have had bad press and sullied reputations because of incidents such as the poisoning in Bhopal and the oil spill in Alaska have faced serious problems. The market value of Union Carbide and Exxon stocks were depressed even though the basic products supplied had not changed. Good reputation enhances business, while poor reputation can have serious negative consequences.

Every January since 1983, *Fortune* has published corporation reputation rankings, obtained from a survey of thousands of executives, outside directors, and financial analysts who are asked to rate the reputations of approximately two to three hundred large firms. The companies are rated on eight key attributes: quality of management; quality of products or services; innovativeness; value as a long-term investment; financial soundness; ability to attract, develop, and keep talented people; community and environmental responsibility; and use of corporate assets.

Chapter 2 will summarize and discuss the results of these surveys. For example, it is interesting to note that in total return (price appreciation and divided yield) to investors, the companies with the highest reputation do not always perform outstandingly well. This suggests that the risk/return tradeoff observed in finance has application here. That is, investing in high-reputation firms and being unwilling to accept risk implies a willingness to accept less return. We will examine the implications (for investment managers as well as corporations) of findings such as these. We will also discuss some individual cases of drastic changes in reputation rankings and speculate on the explanations of sudden surges or drops. The *Fortune* articles provide numerous examples of such happenings. These studies have been published annually for the past nine years. We compare these studies, analyze what factors they evaluate, and examine what has happened over the years to the concepts of reputation and to the firms that were in the high and low categories. In addition, we shall point out some areas where improvements might be made in the *Fortune* Reputation Studies.

In chapter 3 we shall look at other important research on corporate reputation. This research is important in that it shows that some popular conceptions—conceptions built up over time—regarding reputation may actually be *mis*conceptions. For example, Thomas R. King (1989) reports that consumers, for the most part, are not impressed by ads in which celebrities pitch products. According to King, Madison Avenue continues to parade out more and more stars, but he cites some recent research to indicate that such a parade may be to no avail.

Traditionally, it has been thought that financial factors are the chief determinants of stock price, but now market watchers are beginning to investigate other avenues. For example, Claude Rosenberg, Jr., general partner of RCM Capital Management, has his firm comb the country for information from noncorporate sources—distributors, retailers, customers, supplies, and competitors—to evaluate a firm. The network numbers 13,000 sources, including cardiologists, insurance agents, department store managers, and travel agents. Many of these people are performing the function of reputation evaluators. The existence of the network is recognition of the fact that the intangible factor of reputation has a lot to do with the future success or failure of the firm and perhaps even of the industry.

In addition to the *Fortune* studies, the academic community has published a number of research studies. These works have focused on such factors as how reputation relates to economic performance (Sobol and Farrelly 1988; Margulies 1979), relative company size (Sobol and Farrelly 1988), succession systems (Friedman 1986), and reputation formation (Dejong, Forsythe, and Lundholm 1985; Miller 1982). Chapter 3 will summarize the findings of these studies to explore how reputation relates to economic, political, and social factors. In addition, the importance of corporate reputation in the local, national, and international framework will be studied. From this and other sources, in chapters 4 and 5 we will distill ideas on how to build and maintain a good reputation.

Although everyone connected with a firm should pay attention to personal effects on corporate reputation, there are two groups of people for whom maintenance of a good reputation is crucial. These are the public relations personnel responsible for building and maintaining corporate reputation and the CEOs who must define, enhance, and nurture the corporate image. In chapters 4 and 5 we will interview a sample of people in these two areas to find what they think good corporate reputation means, how they evaluate reputation, and what economic, social, and political value this reputation has. We will particularly focus on their suggestions of methods to build a good corporate image. What is the future of corporate reputation building? What will be the important criteria for the 1990s?

Chapter 4 will look at the public relations specialists' role in building corporate image. Today many of them are at the forefront of management. Their positions have expanded from media relations coordinators to marketing developers and image shapers. Where does their input begin? How long has their company had a public relations person/department? How is their role defined and evaluated? Who are they responsible to and what are they responsible for? How has their position changed over the past decade? What do they see changing in the future? What will remain the same? How do they define corporate image? How can a company build a good corporate image? How can a company evaluate its image among potential customers, its internal workings, its community, and other areas it may affect? Which companies have done an outstanding job building corporate image? What is the future of this area? Where does the public relations plan fit into the overall business plan?

Today's business leader faces an extremely competitive environment, an environment that not only demands technical and management skills of a leader, but also requires that leaders be managers and public relations specialists. The mythical rainmaker has disappeared from corporate America to be replaced with a corporate image conscious management. Building and maintaining corporate image has become a shared responsibility.

Although this responsibility is shared there are still two groups that carry the bulk of the responsibility. CEOs and public relations and marketing specialists have the responsibility of devising the approach to building and maintaining corporate image and carrying out the plan. The Suzuki Samari scare, the Tylenol poisonings, the Shuttle crash, the Exxon tanker explosion, and many other incidents have recently put companies' reputations on the line and their leaders in the hot seat. In such situations, companies have a matter of moments in which to save face.

As business deals become more complex, the risk of crises that can destroy corporate image will continue to increase. There are many steps to establishing a corporate image. In chapter 5 we will look at these steps by interviewing CEOs who have coped with these situations. They will be asked to explain how they began their corporate image-building program, how they have coped, what they will do in the future, what they think is the most important factor in building a good reputation, and what consumers can expect to see in the marketplace of the future. The public relations/marketing staff is responsible for the behind-the-scene preparation and sometimes they go before the public; more often than not, however, CEOs are left with the last word. They are left with the opportunity to put the finishing touches on an image-building campaign. Chapter 5 will look at the role CEOs are taking today in the race to build a better corporate image. It will delve into the history of corporate image in their companies, how attitudes have changed over the past ten years, and what the CEOs see in the future.

In our surveys of PR specialists and CEOs we explore what a good corporate image can do for a company. Reputation can be assessed in four areas—labor, product/service sales, finance, and community. In the labor area a good reputation may help to create lower wage rates, less expensive benefit plans, larger selection of potential employees, better quality of workers, and increased loyalty. It turns out that CEOs and PR specialists differ on what they think a good reputation will enable a firm to do. Nevertheless, they agree that it is important to have a good labor force and a good reputation as an employer. Using the Tavistock criteria for what makes a job attractive, we outline a number of ideas to enhance job attractiveness as well as to improve employee performance. Improved employee performance, particularly in the customer service area, can go a long way toward improving corporate reputation for quality of product, quality of service, and ability to attract and keep workers.

In the *Fortune* surveys respondents pick quality of products and services as the second most important component of corporate reputation. In our survey of CEOs and PR specialists, quality of products and services was chosen as the most important corporate reputation attribute. With the passage of the Malcolm Baldrige National Quality Improvement Act in 1987, which covers awards for companies in manufacturing, service, and small business, there is tremendous interest in quality improvement. The 1990s could well become the decade of quality emphasis as total quality management (TQM) is becoming the motto of industry. Indeed, universities, hospitals, and nonprofit organizations have now asked that the Baldrige quality awards be expanded to cover them. In the first part of chapter 7, we discuss the seven Baldrige criteria and how they have changed since 1987. Using our interview data and ideas from current articles and academic papers, we then describe ways in which firms can improve customer satisfaction (the weightiest criterion in the Baldrige competition). This topic of customer satisfaction has eight subcategories that a company must address in its application for an award: determining customer requirements and expectations; customer relationship management; customer service standards; commitment to customers; complaint resolution for quality improvement; determining customer satisfaction; customer satisfaction results; and customer satisfaction comparison.

If a company can increase customer satisfaction, it will be able to improve its corporate reputation, particularly if it can spread the news of this satisfaction to a wide audience and if it can show that in addition to providing such outstanding products and services, it is a financial success.

Not only does financial soundness help to "cause" a good reputation, but a good reputation can help to "cause" financial soundness. This is because firms with good reputations, enjoying the confidence of the public, will find it easier to raise funds (both debt and equity) to support their activities.

Chapter 8 contains ideas on what firms should do in both good and bad times. These suggestions arise from our surveys of CEOs and PR specialists and from recent articles in the current business journals and books. Such ideas as ways to research financial reputation, caring for shareholders' rights, and ways of keeping a corporation in the public eye even in bad times are covered. Other "bad times" strategies include quick and confident response to bad news and the establishment of a crisis control center.

In chapters 6–8 we look at ways to enhance corporate reputation as an employer, as a manufacturer and purveyor of quality products and services, and as a financial manager. Another very important area where a company must present its reputation is in the community. In order to advertise and improve its reputation, the company must make constant efforts to determine its identity. Once identity has been established, the firm can work on increasing visibility.

Some ways to increase visibility are taking a stand on an important issue, or contributing funds, labor, sponsorship, or goods to important and relevant causes. Examples of ways that firms have harmonized their image with community activities are presented in chapter 9.

In addition to domestic identity, in an increasingly globalized market firms must consider their international image. In chapter 9 considerations about global image are covered. Also, ways of conveying this image to the media are discussed. Finally, the constant assessment and re-evaluation of corporate image are presented.

The success or failure of the modern-day corporation is determined by both non-financial and financial factors. Information is smoothly and quickly transmitted; the latest computer wizardry is increasingly able to digest and make use of qualitative as well as quantitative data. For example, unusual corporate restructurings dominate the global financial scene. We may think of these restructurings as unpredictable, merely because we do not see anything in the numbers (sales, earnings, assets) that can explain what is behind the deal. In many of these cases, the hidden asset of reputation may be a major explanatory variable. Reputation is an asset that does not appear on the balance sheet, yet its real value may be greater than that of all the other assets combined! All of this means that forward-looking executives will want to learn all they can about this important intangible asset. Academic and practitioner research on corporate reputation is examined in search of past trends. Public relations executives and chief executive officers are interviewed in order to get some present background on the topic. Reflections on these findings by the authors will provide some input for the future—for developing reputation building in the 1990s and beyond. In chapter 10 our comprehensive study of previous research and the surveys of CEOs and public relations specialists will be summarized and integrated and used to develop a discussion list of actions that might be taken to improve corporate reputation.

CHAPTER 2

Review of *Fortune* Corporate Reputation Studies

It helps you with customers, suppliers, and employees. Your
reputation is everything and should be protected at any cost.
—David Glass, CEO of Wal-Mart Stores,
quoted in "America's Most Admired Corporations,"
Fortune (January 29, 1990: 58)

Recognizing the importance of reputation, *Fortune* runs an annual survey to determine corporate reputation for a sample of the
largest U.S. corporations. The survey is conducted in the fall of
each year and the results are published in January of the following
year. The first of these annual surveys was conducted in the fall of
1982 and published in January 1983. The most recent was done in
the fall of 1990 and published in January 1991. (We will refer to
surveys by the year in which the results were published.)

Times and evaluations have changed over the years. In each of
the first four surveys, IBM emerged with the highest reputation
but was replaced by Merck in the last five surveys. By the time
of the 1990 survey, IBM was in thirty-second place.

Fortune's methodology is quite straightforward. A sample (varying from six to eight thousand) of financial analysts, high executives, and outside directors are polled and asked to rate companies in their own industry. A scale of 0 (poor) to 10 (excellent) is used by *Fortune*, and the rating is done on eight attributes:

1. Financial soundness
2. Value as a long-term investment
3. Wise use of corporate assets
4. Innovativeness
5. Ability to attract, develop, and keep talented people
6. Quality of products or services
7. Quality of management
8. Community and environmental responsibility

The final rating on corporate reputation, for each firm, is the average score on each of these eight attributes. The first survey covered two hundred companies; the survey now covers over three hundred firms. (Table 2.1 provides some basic statistics on the nine *Fortune* studies published thus far.)

Reputation is an intangible, impossible-to-define asset, so a reputation survey is a difficult project to tackle. Accordingly, it seems good that *Fortune* considers a list of eight determinants, some of which are financial, some of which are nonfinancial. This is important, because often the whole story about a company cannot be told through financial factors alone.

Also, on a positive note, there is some variety (actually three categories—executives, directors, analysts) in the type of respondent canvassed. The respondents must be knowledgeable, since they rate only firms in their own industry, and only the largest firms at that. Since the same type of audience is canvassed each year and average scores are produced, the historical record of rankings should be meaningful. Reputation is ever-changing; the *Fortune* survey enables one to compare, from year to year, the

Table 2.1
Fortune **Surveys of Corporate Reputation, 1983–1991**

Year of Survey Publication	Number of Companies Covered	Number of Questionnaires Sent Out	Response Rate
1983	200	6,000	51%
1984	250	7,000	50%
1985	250	8,000	52%
1986	292	8,000	50%
1987	300	8,200	50%
1988	306	8,000	44%
1989	305	8,000	Not given
1990	305	8,000	Not given
1991	306	"more than 8,000"	Not given

rank assigned to a substantial number of firms. Then, aided by the "history" of the rankings, one can search historically and attempt to explain the change in rankings through the history of various "happenings" that affect the firm (both financial and nonfinancial). And the firm is set within its own industry, facilitating comparisons among firms in the same industry. In the world of investing, there are many sources that are purely financial and many sources that provide anecdotal evidence on nonfinancial factors. But reputation is an amalgam of both, so reputation rankings such as those provided by *Fortune* should be valuable.

Table 2.2 summarizes some important overall results of the *Fortune* studies. This table lists the twenty-nine firms that, at one time or another, have been rated among the top ten firms in terms of reputation. Merck, which has topped the survey for the past five years, is the only one of the twenty-nine firms to make the top ten for all nine years of the survey. IBM had the top spot for the first four years, slipped to seventh place in the fifth survey, and has not made the top ten since then (receiving ranks of 32, 34, 45, and 32 in the last four surveys).

Only five companies have maintained status in the top ten for the last three years: Merck; Pepsico (showing a steady improvement: ranked No. 5 in 1991, up a notch from the previous

Table 2.2

Companies Ranked in the Top Ten in *Fortune* Reputation Studies, 1983–1991

Ranks and (Scores) for Nine Surveys

	1983	1984	1985	1986	1987	1988	1989	1990	1991
Anheuser-Busch								9 (7.96)	
AT&T									9 (7.92)
Boeing	6 (7.91)	8 (7.91)	6 (7.96)				8 (8.03)		
Coca-Cola		10 (7.79)	7 (7.80)	6 (7.90)	3 (7.99)			8 (8.15)	6 (8.12)
Digital Equipment		9 (7.87)	2 (8.34)	4 (7.98)					
Dow Jones	7 (7.70)								
DuPont						3 (8.24)		10 (7.93)	
Eastman Kodak	4 (8.02)	2 (8.35)	3 (8.31)	3 (8.07)	9 (7.84)				
Eli Lilly									10 (7.90)
Exxon			9 (7.72)				6 (8.05)		
GE				9 (7.72)					
General Mills	9 (7.54)	7 (7.96)	8 (7.79)						
Herman Miller	10 (7.52)				10 (7.84)		9 (7.99)		
Hewlett Packard	2 (8.26)	3 (8.24)	5 (8.08)	1 (8.31)	7 (7.91)				
IBM	1 (8.26)	1 (8.53)	1 (8.44)		8 (7.86)				
Johnson & Johnson					4 (7.95)				8 (8.01)
J. P. Morgan	3 (8.14)	5 (8.15)		10 (7.71)	2 (8.02)	8 (8.03)			
Liz Claiborne						5 (8.14)			10 (7.90)
Merck	5 (7.92)	4 (8.17)	10 (7.66)	5 (7.91)	1 (8.38)	1 (9.00)	1 (8.87)	1 (8.90)	1 (8.86)
Pepsico							7 (8.04)	6 (8.16)	5 (8.19)
Philip Morris						7 (8.07)	4 (8.15)	2 (8.78)	
Procter & Gamble				8 (7.79)		4 (8.15)		4 (8.37)	3 (8.42)
RJR Nabisco				7 (7.80)		9 (7.90)			
Rubbermaid					5 (7.94)	2 (8.29)	2 (8.41)	3 (8.42)	2 (8.58)
Shell Oil					6 (7.91)		10 (7.96)		
SmithKline Beckman									
3M			4 (8.13)	2 (8.12)		6 (8.10)	3 (8.18)	5 (8.21)	6 (8.12)
Time	8 (7.66)								
Wal-Mart Stores		6 (7.99)				9 (7.90)	5 (8.12)	6 (8.16)	4 (8.35)

* Years refer to dates of publication of survey results.

The first digit in each column represents the rank for the firm.

The numbers in parentheses represent the average rating for the 8 dimensions studied.

year); Rubbermaid (in positions No. 2 or No. 3); 3M (No. 6 in the latest survey); and Wal-Mart Stores (No. 4, up from No. 6 in 1990).

Not only being in the top spot, but staying there, is recognized as an important goal at Merck. P. Roy Vagelos, the M.D. who runs Merck, has commented, "Because we're in the business of improving people's health, our reputation is probably more important than the amount of money we make" (Baig 1987: 20). Reputation is, of course, one of the prime ingredients for making money. According to Vagelos (Schultz 1988: 38), Merck's status on the *Fortune* survey "did great things" for the morale of the company and for recruiting; name recognition on campuses produced "super" recruiting results.

Merck, may not, at present, be a household word but it is fast becoming one. Recently, it made the news by proposing a plan to make its prescription drugs available at lower prices to Medicaid patients. According to the *Wall Street Journal* (Winslow 1990: B1, B4), "The Merck plan could be both a political and marketing coup for the nation's leading drug company, and it could save Medicaid programs nationwide a total of $30 million a year, based on Merck's current sales." That is the beauty of being on top—the firm can afford to try some new activities that have the potential to enhance its reputation even further. It is an application of the old adage that "the rich get richer." Lesser firms may have some ideas about new things to try but may not have the resources, the cost of capital, and/or the "reputation" to attempt some new strategies. A willingness to accept risk is necessary to get to the top. It is a constant challenge to be on top and yet not be complacent but continue to take the risks that will keep you there. Merck seems willing to take these risks. Tangible evidence of the importance of innovation is the size of the research and development budget of Merck. In 1990 (Sprout 1991: 57), the firm spent $855 million— about 11 percent of 1990s sales and nearly 10 percent of the entire U.S. pharmaceutical R&D budget.

Three qualities, according to *Fortune* (Davenport 1989: 68), mark companies consistently regarded most highly by their peers:

earnings growth, product innovation, and ambitious operating goals. "Merck's earnings per share have risen at least 25% for 14 consecutive quarters. . . . Rubbermaid . . . has met or surpassed CEO Stanley Gault's goal of 15% annual sales and earnings growth for three years running. Pepsico has spent some $8 billion on acquisitions since 1985 and increased earnings at a compound annual rate of over 20% while doing so" (Smith 1990: 58, 62).

3M, a company among the top ten for six of the last nine years, provides a good example of product innovation. *Fortune* cites one analyst, Theresa Gusman of Salomon Brothers, as saying: "3M gives people an environment in which they can create, and they just come up with brilliant idea after brilliant idea" (Davenport 1989: 70). In 1990 (Smith 1990: 62), the same analyst wrote of 3M, "This is a company that develops a whole new process for making Scotch tape, even when it already dominates the market. They are amazing." It is clear that product innovation does not just happen; it is the result of good management strategy in finding and motivating creative people. It is also a good indication of how the *Fortune* attributes of good reputation overlap somewhat; consider, for example, innovativeness and the ability to attract, develop, and keep talented people. These qualities really go hand in hand.

Sam M. Walton, founder and chair of Wal-Mart Stores, a company on the top ten list for the past four years (in fact, since it first became eligible to be included in the survey as one of the ten retailers—see 1988 survey, p. 34) recently provided a good example of ambitious operating goals by saying that he thought the company could quintuple sales to about $125 billion by the year 2000. He appears to have the employee backing with which to succeed. It was reported in the *Wall Street Journal* that at the 1990 annual meeting "the Arkansas billionaire had the fire and vigor of a revival preacher as he led more than 8,000 shareholders and employees in a series of call-and-response cheers. 'Can we do it,' he shouted. 'Yes we can,' they roared back" (Tomsho 1990: B9C). There is a lot in recent management literature about a growing gap between managers and workers, a gap that must be bridged by companies hoping for success in the 1990s. Wai-Mart appears to have bridged that gap. The publicity associated with this cannot but help enhance the reputation of the firm (Tomsïno 1990: B9C).

What seems to characterize the top firms is an unmatched consistency of success. They do not achieve an absolutely fantastic return in any one year, but their earning power is constant and sustainable and thus inspires confidence. In a changing, unpredictable world, they are solid entities that investors can cling to. Nancy J. Perry (1984: 50) indicated that 1947 was the most recent year that any of the most admired group lost money. And, of the companies in the top ten for the second time in 1984, only Merck had ever reported an unprofitable year, back in 1921. Patricia Sellers (1985: 18) indicated that "None of the top ten has had an annual loss in 35 years or more." More recently, Ellen Schultz (1988: 34, 37) indicated that during the stock market crash of October 1987, reputation was an important determinant of how far firms fell: "From the beginning of 1987 to December 11, the median total return to shareholders (dividends plus capital gains or losses) for all 306 companies surveyed fell 5.9%. By contrast, the median loss for the ten most admired companies came to less than 1%, and the loss for the ten least admired hit a wallet-thinning 28.8%." It is a safety that comes with a hefty price. Top reputation firms, for the most part, armed with a proven record of success and safety also come with high price tags. This is a true application of the old maxim, "there's no such thing as a free lunch." One has to pay for quality in any market.

This may explain why in total return (a measure combining price appreciation and dividend yield) to investors, top reputation firms do not always perform outstandingly well. Cynthia Hutton (1986: 16) reports that the top ten's ten-year median total return to investors—dividends plus the stock's price appreciation—was 14.9 percent, lower than that of the *Fortune* 500 (a return of 18.7 percent). It was, though, a lot higher than the return of the least admired group—4.6 percent!

The stocks of the most admired group are safe, secure stocks, and the prices are relatively high. This indicates that there is general agreement (a high evaluation) of these stocks. The way to make money in the market is by not agreeing with everyone but by disagreeing and being right.

Top reputation firms also seem to have the knack of "bouncing back" after disasters that could be the ruin of other firms. A recent case in point in Coca-Cola, which was forced to end its MagiCans promotion after a few weeks. The promotion was supposed to increase sales; the plan was that some "lucky" consumers, on opening certain cans, would find cash rather than Coke. Unfortunately, the firm had lots of trouble with malfunctioning cans; and, although consumers were instructed not to drink the liquid in the "cash" cans, this was not always understood. The promotion came to a quick end. This experiment was certainly innovative but not very successful.

Coca-Cola has been among the top ten in reputation five times. Even though it has experienced some glitches in the recent past—not only the MagiCans but also with the Classic Coke controversy of several years ago—Coca-Cola recovers quickly; it bounces back and misses barely a beat. It seems undeterred by the failure of recent promotions. Coca-Cola may have had a momentary lapse in juggling innovation and consumer needs, but it has been quick to pick up the dropped ball.

It is interesting to note how certain negative events affect the reputation rankings. According to *Fortune*, the reputation of Johnson & Johnson was hurt by the deaths in September 1982 of seven people in Chicago who swallowed Tylenol capsules that someone had packed with cyanide; the company quickly and honestly dealt with the tragedy, withdrawing the drug at a pretax cost of over $100 million (Perry 1984: 54). In the survey taken in the fall of 1982 and published in January 1983, it scored first among the 250 companies for community responsibility. Chair James Burke, noting that Johnson & Johnson also had to withdraw the pain reliever Zomax from the market, commented, "We really cashed in on the reputation of 90 years of this company".

The same high level of responsibility seemingly was not attributed to Exxon after the Valdez incident. The rank for Exxon dropped from 6 to 110 in the *Fortune* survey published in 1990. There seemed to be a haughty quality to Exxon's defense that, more than anything else, annoyed the public.

Although the *Fortune* reputation surveys may be very informative, they really do not help to define reputation. In essence, definition is done by the survey design, which lists the eight "predetermined" attributes of corporate reputation. Theoretically, one can respond to the survey, although one disagrees with one or more of the eight attributes of reputation as defined by *Fortune*. Therefore, even after thoroughly analyzing the *Fortune* studies, one is still left with the question: what is corporate reputation? M. W. Blume, writing in the *Journal of Finance* twenty years ago, said about the concept of risk that there is no general agreement on how to measure it, but there is general agreement that it is important. The same notion applies to corporate reputation. People agree that it is important and valuable to a firm, but there is no general agreement on what it really means or how it is measured. Ask ten different people, and you may get ten different answers. *Fortune,* however, does ask respondents each year to pick, of the eight attributes, which are the most important in determining reputation. Alison L. Sprout (1991: 52) reports that "Every year more than 80% of the respondents to *Fortune*'s survey pick quality of management as paramount. But other criteria have been growing in popularity. The quality of a company's products or services, considered the second most significant factor ever since the survey began nearly a decade ago, is narrowing the gap with management." These two qualities seem more inclusive than any of the others. If the quality of management is high, the company should be able to cope with both the expected and unexpected, and other attributes of reputation should fall into place. Likewise, high-quality products and services should be important in attaining and maintaining a good reputation. At the same time, it is important to note that, in the latest survey (ibid), "the number of respondents citing responsibility to the community and environment as the most important standard for judging a corporate reputation has doubled." Times change, and firms that want to build and preserve a good reputation need to keep up with those changes. A firm that does not keep up with the times may end up meeting an obsolete standard.

The lack of an attempt to define reputation is not the only negative aspect of the *Fortune* survey. Only the largest companies in each industry are covered. While these results may be interesting, perhaps even more interesting would be results related to mid-sized and smaller firms. After all, larger firms make the news a lot anyway; it is harder to get information and rate the reputation of small firms. (This is a circular problem; many respondents would probably not be knowledgeable enough to rate the reputation of smaller firms.)

As already mentioned, there is some variety in the type of respondent canvassed by *Fortune*. One wonders, however, if even this variety is enough. Each company is evaluated by respondents in the same industry. This is both bad news and good news. In some cases, the evaluators may be too close to do a truly accurate job of evaluating. They may not always spot potential problems as quickly as an outsider could or recognize contributions of "upstarts." Ultimately, companies, through the stock market, are evaluated by a general audience; an industry-specific audience may not be the best.

Results of the latest survey cast some light on the issue of industry-specific evaluators. Philip Morris, when its main source of revenue was tobacco products, had done quite well in the survey. As shown in table 2.2, Philip Morris had moved from seventh place in the survey published in 1988, to fourth place in 1989, to second place in 1990. It was somewhat startling to see this increase in reputation, given the ever-increasing evidence of the health dangers of smoking to both smokers and nonsmokers. It could not be denied that the financial performance of the firm is worthy of admiration. As indicated by *Fortune*, Philip Morris had achieved an annual average return (dividends plus appreciation in the stock) of 30.1 percent over the years 1979–1989. And in 1990, as indicated by *Fortune*, it continued to perform spectacularly well; net income for the first nine months of the year was up by 28 percent.

In the latest survey, however, Philip Morris (having acquired Kraft in 1988 was categorized as a food rather than a tobacco firm, and thus faced a new set of evaluators. The result was that Philip Morris slipped from second to seventy-ninth place. As Alison Sprout stated in *Fortune* (1991: 52):

Philip Morris's new judges in the food business didn't think much of its best-known product—cigarettes. The director of one food company put it bluntly: "Anyone in the tobacco business must be severely downgraded." Another executive wrote, "I downgraded companies with political action committees, products that kill, and those insensitive to 'green' issues." Philip Morris's scores for product quality and community and environmental responsibility fell accordingly, accounting for most of its drop on the list.

This is in spite of the fact that Philip Morris engages in a lot of public service announcements. In recent ones, they invite readers to "Join Philip Morris in support of the National Archives' celebration of the 200th anniversary of the Bill of Rights." They go on to offer free copies of the Bill of Rights upon request. But apparently such ads were not enough to counteract negative reaction to their tobacco products—at least the reactions of their food industry judges. At the same time, we have to wonder how relevant the view of this specific group of judges is. Is this the reputation rating that really "counts?" Is it representative enough?

Among those not canvassed are the following groups: customers, suppliers, scientific experts, trend watchers, employees below the executive level, and neighborhood groups. Ultimately, of course, the "vote" of these parties will count in sales and financial results of future periods; and, admittedly, it would be difficult to get a representative sample of these groups. Nevertheless, their importance cannot be forgotten. This seems especially true in the present age, as evidenced by the fact that market watchers are beginning to investigate avenues other than financial ones. For example, Grassroots Research, organized in 1984 by money manager Claude Rosenberg, Jr., concentrates on getting investment data from nontraditional sources. As reported recently in the *Wall Street Journal* (White 1990: C1, C27), "Compared with the number-crunching and company forecasts that are at the heart of traditional investment research, the Grassroots operation collects its data from the likes of cosmetics buyers, sneaker salesmen, travel agents and even town landfill operators (who know if dumping fees are rising to the detriment of waste disposal companies). Company officials are almost never queried."

Here we have another set of reputation evaluators, none of whom are directly related to the companies being evaluated. What is important about this approach is that it stresses what is happening now, rather than what has happened in the past. It has been said that Rosenberg instituted his unique approach to investment research several years ago when Atari Corporation stock took an unexpected plunge. In hindsight, Rosenberg saw that the nosedive was predictable considering the big buildup in inventories that had occurred at Atari. Apparently this convinced Rosenberg that there were lots of untapped sources for investment information.

Interestingly, individual investors are using a similar approach. Earl C. Gottschalk, Jr. (1990: C1, C2) states that some individual investors are scoring big profits by uncovering winning stocks in their own locales, long before they are discovered by investment professionals. According to Gottschalk, their secret is "Focusing on up-and-coming companies close to home, while avoiding the pitfalls of local boosterism and small-stock volatility." He quotes Susanne Heimbuch, a public relations consultant and a believer in investing in local stocks, who suggests a simple but effective way to determine if the proposed firm is hiring or laying off people: "You can drop by and count the cars in the parking lot."

Only top executives are surveyed in the *Fortune* poll. Middle management and lower-level employees are excluded. If top management can adequately speak for the industry, this exclusion is not a problem; but recently the ability of top managers to do so had been questioned. If middle managers are not being motivated as they should be and if they do not share the goals, enthusiasm, and vision of top executives, then the predictions, plans, and evaluations of high executives may not be all that accurate.

Distributors, another group not directly queried by *Fortune*, are also important in evaluating reputation, as indicated recently by Peter Drucker (1900: A12):

Changes in distributive channels may not matter much to GNP and macro-economics. But they should be a major concern of every business. Yet they are very difficult to predict. What's worse, they do not show up in reports and statistics until they have gone very far. To be able to anticipate changes in distributive channels and in where customers buy (and how, which is equally important) one has to be in the marketplace, has to watch customers, and non-customers, has to ask "dumb questions."

It may be the case that the groups surveyed by *Fortune* are not quite representative of the market.

It seems ironic that, in our economy, we have progressed to a very sophisticated system of financial information disclosure; but since this information is freely available to all, investors must look to something else in order to get the edge. So, in a way, we are back to the beginning, in a scenario where each investor has to ferret out individual information in an attempt to achieve above-average success in investing. Yet at the same time we have progressed to the point of recognizing that financial disclosure tells only a small portion of the story of how a company is doing. For large, publicly held companies, the basic financial information is available to all; but investors see that they must move beyond this limited data into the realm of "soft," subjective, hard-to-assess nonfinancial factors. This is an area where corporate reputation can spell success or failure for the firm.

The *Fortune* studies are of interest because they give a large amount of data on corporate reputation; for some firms, a nine-year history of corporation reputation scores is provided. But even more important, these studies provoke thought, analysis, study, and discussion on an elusive and intriguing topic that market watchers cannot explain by the use of numbers (earnings, dividends, price data) alone.

CHAPTER 3

Academic Studies of Corporate Reputation: Origins and Effects

In a recent interview by Gary Putka in the *Wall Street Journal*, (1990: B1, B2) Richard Cyert, president of Carnegie Mellon, says:

Foreign companies are ahead of U.S. companies in recognizing the value of American university research. They have a better feel for being able to read something and transfer that knowledge to applications. If you go into a Japanese operation, you'll find as much as two to three hours a day is spent by supervisors and others in production in reading the journals and trying to get ideas that can be applied. Almost every idea they have adopted has been in the academic literature. The same thing is true of the Germans.

In chapter 2, we pointed out the strengths and weaknesses of the corporate reputation ratings published annually by *Fortune*. Even though these measures have some problems, as do all rating scales, they provide an excellent standard that can be used to study the behavior and characteristics of firms with "good" reputations. And indeed a number of academic researchers have studied firms with high and low rankings according to the overall

Fortune ratings. Others have looked at factors related to individual reputation items (such as community responsibility or ability to attract and keep good workers) and financial reputation to see how reputations arise or how firms with high and low reputations differ. In this chapter, we will look at current academic research to see how high or low corporate reputation relates to financial performance of the firm, to relative size of the firm, and to other behavior. These studies will help us see the underlying factors that influence corporate reputation and will thus aid companies in their effort to build their reputation.

High corporate reputation may lead to the ability to hire outstanding people for top-level positions (Chajet 1989), the ability to raise needed capital (Margulies 1979), and the ability to operate not only in local markets but in global marketplaces (Chajet 1989). Sales also often depend on company reputation. For example, in the microcomputer market even though IBM did not have the most innovative or cheapest personal computer, it initially made rapid market inroads because of company reputation (Verity 1984).

STUDIES THAT USE THE *FORTUNE* REPUTATION RATINGS

The Sobol–Farrelly Study

Marion G. Sobol and Gail Farrelly pursue the interesting issue of how corporate reputation is formed. These authors consider whether corporate reputation is merely a reflection of the financial performance of the company or whether it is based on other, less measurable factors. This is, of course, a difficult task; in fact, one could argue that the ultimate answer can never be fully discovered, because it resides in the psyches of the people making the evaluations! Using the *Fortune* survey and data from *Moody's Handbook of Common Stock* (1982), Sobol and Farrelly test the following issues:

- To what extent do each of the eight attributes of corporate reputation relate to past financial performance (measured by earnings per share, price/earnings ratio, and average yield)?
- What is the lag between good financial performance and good corporate reputation?
- Does relative size of net income (relative market share) in a particular industry relate to corporate reputation?

In this section of the chapter, we devote a good deal of attention to the methodology and findings of Sobol and Farrelly. We do this for a number of reasons. This is an important study, since it includes all eight attributes covered in the *Fortune* studies. It may suggest some ideas for future research to academic readers. It may help managerial practitioners come to a better understanding of what goes into their own corporate reputation ratings and provoke thought as to how these ratings may be improved. Also, examining perceptions of corporate reputation and linking these perceptions to financial characteristics of firms may lead to better ways for finance professionals to make investment decisions that will bring high returns to their clients.

As previously mentioned, respondents were asked in the *Fortune* survey to rate the companies on a scale from 0 (poor) to 10 (excellent), in terms of each of eight key attributes of reputation. The final rating on corporate reputation, for each firm, is the average score for the eight attributes. Some survey data provided by the editor of *Fortune* and not provided to the general public in the *Fortune* article permitted tests with the individual scores on each of the eight attributes for each of the two hundred firms.[1] This "extra" data facilitated the analyses of the components of corporate reputation and not just the one average figure.

Data were collected on factors related to financial performance for the years 1973–1982. Three measures were chosen as criteria of financial performance. *Earnings per share* (EPS) is the net income divided by the number of shares outstanding. It is a figure that reveals accounting profit but does not take into account stock price. On the other hand, the *price/earnings (P/E) ratio* takes into account both price and earnings. In theory, this ratio reflects how much an investor will pay for one dollar of earnings. The brighter the perceived future of the firm, the higher the amount an investor will be willing to pay and the higher the price/earnings ratio. The *average yield* reflects the dividend per share divided by the average price of common stock; it is thus a measure of the current return (in cash) an investment is generating. Also, the net income for 1981 (the year prior to the *Fortune* survey) for each of the firms was collected from *Moody's*. Thus, the relative standing (market share) of firms within industry groupings could be ranked.

For each of the eight attributes of corporate reputation, it is interesting to see which of the thirty data points (EPS [1973–1982], P/E ratio [1973–1982], and average yield for the ten years prior to the survey [1973–1982]) are significant in "explaining" the rankings. The eight attributes of corporate reputation fall into two categories: financial and nonfinancial. The first three attributes (financial soundness, value as a long-term investment, and the use of corporate assets) are designated by Sobol and Farrelly as financial attributes and the last five (innovativeness; ability to attract, develop, and keep talented people; quality of products or services; quality of management; and community and environmental responsibility) as nonfinancial.

Financial Factors

In the analysis of what affects *financial soundness*, the three financial ratios discussed above were related to financial soundness for the ten years prior to the *Fortune* ranking. As shown in table 3.1, the breakdown of these six significant variables is in order as follows: P/E ratio 1976, P/E ratio 1978, average yield 1977, P/E ratio 1981, EPS 1974 (negatively related), EPS 1979. Thus, the price/earnings ratios in the five years prior to estimation of financial soundness are especially crucial measures. This study of the factors that affect financial soundness indicate that there is a lag averaging about 4 years between financial influences and the actual condition of financial soundness ratings

Table 3.1
Financial Factors Related to Corporate Reputation Indexes, *Fortune* Corporate Reputation Factors, 1982 (for all 200 companies)

(1) Financial Soundness	(2) Value As a Long Term Investment	(3) Wise Use of Corporate Assets	(4) Innovativeness	(5) Ability to Attract, Develop and Keep Talented People	(6) Quality of Product or Services	(7) Quality of Management	(8) Responsibility to Community & Environment
PE '76 (.149)*	PE '76 (.120)	PE '78 (.117)	PE '78 (.148)	PE '74 (.146)	PE '78 (.143)	PE '78 (.110)	PE '76 (.143)
PE '78 (.206)	EPS '74 (.183)	PE '81 (.174)	EPS '74 (-) (.198)	PE '79 (.202)	PE '76 (.208)	PE '81 (.183)	AY '81 (.251)
AY '77 (.246)	EPS '76 (.239)	AY '81 (.203)	AY '79 (.242)	PE '81 (.238)	PE '81 (.242)	PE '76 (.204)	PE '81 (.301)
PE '81 (.298)	AY '78 (.283)	EPS '74 (.238)	PE '74 (.278)	PE '76 (.267)	AY '78 (.289)	AY '78 (.228)	PE '73 (.332)
EPS '74 (-) (.324)	PE '81 (.314)	PE '76 (.272)	EPS '80 (.304)	AY '78 (.301)		EPS '74 (-) (.263)	PE '77 (-) (.350)
EPS '79 (.380)	AY '81 (.333)	EPS '81 (.311)	PE '79 (.324)	EPS '74 (-) (.335)		EPS '81 (.309)	AY '77 (.367)
		AY '77 (.345)	PE '82 (.340)	EPS '76 (.369)			
				AY '81 (.383)			

*The figures in brackets represent the coefficients of determination for the relationship of this variable with the corporate factor. These coefficients are additive so that (.206) for PE '78 for the financial soundness factor is a result of .149 for PE '76 and an additional .057 when PE '78 is added. The most important variable is first on the ladder of significant variables. For example, PE '76 is most important in explaining Financial Soundness.

Source: Sobol, Marion G. and Gail Farrelly, "Corporate Reputation: A Function of Relative Size of Financial Performance?" Review of Business and Economic Research, Fall, 1988, p. 48.

for the corporate reputation scale. Note that in table 3.1, the most important variable is first on the ladder of significant variables.

Just as the price/earnings ratio in 1976 was the most important variable related to financial soundness $(R^2 = .149)^2$ in 1982, this same variable shows the strongest relationship to *value as a long-term investment* $(R^2 = .120)$. The price/earnings ratio for 1981 is the fifth most important variable in the explanation of value as a long-term investment and fourth most important in explaining financial soundness. Earnings per share for 1974 and 1976 are positively related to value. Finally the average yield for 1978 and 1981 was related to long-term value. The six variables explained .380 of the variations in long-run financial value. Once again we see a one- to seven-year lag in financial variables and overall reputation. It evidently takes a while for good financial performance to be reflected in good corporate reputation ratings.

Comparing *wise use of corporate assets* with price/earnings ratio, earnings per share, and average yield for the years 1973–1982, the most significant variable in this analysis was the price/earnings ratio in 1978. The price/earnings ratio of 1981 also provided a significant—although not quite as important—explanation of the other two financial variables. Thus, wise use of corporate assets can be primarily explained by the price/earnings ratios of 1978 and 1981. Adding the price/earnings ratio of 1981 improved the explanation by 5.7 percent. The next significant variable that was entered was the average yield for 1981. The addition of the average yield for 1981 improved the explanation by almost 3 percent. Then the following were added: earnings per share for 1974, price/earnings ratio in 1976, and earnings per share for 1981. 31.1 percent of wise use of corporate assets could be explained by these six variables. The addition of the earnings per share for 1981 was a 3.9 percent improvement. The last significant variable was the average yield of 1977. This made the total R^2 value .345, which indicated that 34.5 percent of wise use of corporate assets can be explained by these seven variables. This is actually a very high degree of explanation for an economic analysis using multiple regression techniques. All three financial measures for P/E ratio, average yield, and earnings per share 1981, the year prior to the survey, were significant in explaining wise use of corporate assets. The lag between these financial variables and estimates of wise use of resources is smaller than for other variables. It, therefore, seems that most recent financial return measures relate to respondents' impressions of wise asset use.

Nonfinancial Factors

The financial characteristics that influence good corporate reputations have been considered above. The *Fortune* scale gives these only 3/8 of the weight in the calculation of overall corporate reputation. The remaining weight in this index is occupied by the combination of innovativeness, ability to attract, develop, and keep talented people, quality of products or services, quality of management, and corporate responsibility. These managerial decisions reflect the management strategy of the company.

Innovativeness is a very important factor in the long-run success of a business enterprise. Because of the competitive nature of business and the fact that most industries are always making technological improvements, a company will soon fall behind its competitors if it does not spend enough time and money on the development of new ideas and products. For example, the Japanese innovation of smaller, more fuel-efficient cars in a time of rapidly increasing oil prices caused a significant rise in the number of imported Japanese cars in the United States as well as a marked decline in the sales of larger, less fuel-efficient American cars. As Louis A. Girifalco (1982:3) notes, "In general, when a new technology comes along, some firms are able to take advantage of it, while others are not. The rewards for the winners are great, the punishment for the losers is severe."

The question is, how do financial factors relate to innovativeness? In a multiple regression analysis that related the innovativeness ratings of two-hundred companies in the *Fortune Corporate Reputation Survey* to the price/earnings ratios, earnings per share, and average yield percentage of those companies over a ten-year period, there was an indication of a significant relationship between innovativeness and the above measures of financial success. In fact, the seven most significant variables were able to explain 34.0 percent of the total variance. This was about the same percentage that financial factors explained for financial estimates of the firm!

The most significant variable was the price/earnings ratio for 1978 (see table 3.1). It explained 14.8 percent of the total variation, almost half of all the variation explained. Following that was the earnings per share for 1974, which explained another 5 percent of the variation. Note here that the relationship between earnings per share in 1974 and innovativeness is negative. In order to innovate, a firm must often accept high expenses (research and development, for example) that decrease current income but promise future rewards. Note too the time lag; the ploughback in 1974 is correlated to reputation for innovativeness in 1982. The third most important variable was average yield in 1979. The price/earnings ratio for 1974 is the fourth most important variable related to innovativeness. For these innovative companies even though earnings per share were very low, prices stayed high no doubt since investors realized that their money was being used for innovative purposes. Three other important financial figures related to innovativeness were more recent—earnings per share 1980, price/earnings ratio 1979, and price/earnings ratio 1982.

Occasionally innovativeness may necessitate that corporations withhold dividends but generally the financial variables related to innovativeness seem to be the same as those that relate to the general financial success of the firm.

There were eight variables that explained a total of 30 percent of the variation in firms' *ability to maintain good personnel*. The four most important variables related to this ability to attract good personnel were price/earnings ratios for 1974, 1979, 1981, and 1976, respectively (see table 3.1).

In a sense, a price/earnings ratio is a representation of how a market regards corporations. Thus firms with high P/E are regarded as firms with potential for improvement. This may attract new employees and keep good ones.

Only four financial variables related to *product quality* ratings (see table 3.1). These were price/earnings ratio 1978, price/earnings ratio 1976, price/earnings ratio 1981, and average yield 1978. It is interesting to note that current ratings of product quality are primarily rated to price/earnings ratios of previous years. Perhaps price/earnings ratios contain implicit ratings of product quality so that people are willing to pay relatively more for a stock of a company they think will produce a high-quality product.

Quality of management and quality of product seem to be very closely allied in terms of financial factors. The first four variables that explain quality of management ratings are the same as those that explain quality of product rating (see table 3.1). They are price/earnings return 1978, price/earnings return 1976, price/earnings ratio 1981, and average yield 1978. These four factors explain approximately 22.8 percent of quality of management ratings and 28.9 percent of quality of product ratings.

There were two other financial measures that contributed to the explanation of opinions of quality of management. These are earnings per share for 1974, which is negatively related just as it was negatively related to innovation, and financial capabilities of the firm. Often past low earnings may relate to high future earnings in that they represent investment ploughback. A company with good rather than poor management is a management who believes in investment. Recent high earnings also relate positively to quality of management.

The eighth factor considered in the determination of corporate reputation is *responsibility to the environment and community*. Pollution control, product safety, and environmental waste are among the issues considered here. Responsiveness to society's needs was ranked fourteenth place out of forty-four choices as a help in creating favorable corporate image by a 1981 Opinion Research Survey (Miller 1982).

Price/earning ratios are quite important in relation to ratings for corporate responsibility. The price/earnings ratios of 1976 explained 14.3 percent of the ratings. Average yield for 1981 came in second, explaining an additional 11 percent of variation in corporate reputations. Price/earnings ratios for 1981 and 1973 came in next, explaining a total of 8 percent more. Strangely, the price/earnings ratio for 1977 was negatively related to reputation for corporate responsibility. Finally, average yield of 1977 is positively related to corporate reputation for responsibility.

Financial Ratios versus Relative Size of Company Income

We have seen in the previous section that average yield, earnings per share, and price/earnings ratio do relate to overall company reputation and to perceptions of financial soundness. Often there is a two- to four-year lag between these variables and high performance in terms of reputation ranking. A very interesting question concerning reputation ranking is whether reputation is a function of relative size of net income, Rather than performance in the stock market. Are the firms that have the highest income in their fields (the largest market share) the firms that enjoy the best reputations? This is the question studied in the second stage of the Sobol–Farrelly analysis.

Each industry was studied separately, as the net income of food companies, for example, may not be comparable to the net income of office equipment firms. For each industry, the stepwise regression discussed previously was recalculated. One more variable was added—net income for 1981 (the year before the survey). Thus, for each company there were thirty-one data points—the three independent variables (EPS, P/E ratio, and average yield) for the ten years prior to the survey and total net income for 1981. This enabled us to examine, on an industry-by-industry basis, how well these financial performance measures and relative size of net income could "explain" corporate reputation.

Table 3.2
Industries Where Relative Size, P/E Ratio, or Average Yield Are Most Important Variables Related to Overall Corporate Reputation, *Fortune* Data, 1982

Relative Size (Measured by Net Income)	P/E Ratios	Average Yield
1. Petroleum refining (AY)	1. Metal Manufacturing	1. Food
2. Pharmaceutical (AY)	2. Diversified Financial Cos.	
3. Office Equipment and Computers (PE, AY)	3. Commercial Banking Cos.	
4. Industrial & Farm Equipment (PE)	4. Retailing Companies	
5. Chemicals	5. Transportation Cos.	
6. Utilities	6. Electronics & Appliances	
7. Aerospace (PE)		
8. Measuring, Scientific and Photographic Equipment (AY)		

Note: Other variables that were significantly related are denoted in parentheses.

Source: Sobol, Marion G. and Gail Farrelly, "Corporate Reputation: A Function of Relative Size or Financial Performance?" Review of Business and Economic Research, Fall, 1988, p. 49.

The results, summarized in table 3.2, are striking. For eight of the twenty industries studied, the variable most importantly related to overall corporate reputation was the size of net income. For six industries price/earnings ratios were most important; for one industry (food) average yield was most important; and for the remaining five industries financial variables did not significantly affect overall corporate reputation. This all-pervasive influence of size of net income is shown by the fact that the coefficients of determination in a number of the industry-specific regression equations are quite impressive. For example, with the inclusion of the net income variable, we can explain a high percentage of the variation in corporate reputation rankings—90 percent in the diversified financial industry, 83 percent in two industries (office equipment; measuring, scientific, photographic equipment), 80 percent in the aerospace industry, and more than 70 percent in each of the following four industries: petroleum refining, chemicals, utilities, and transportation. This finding about the correlation of relative market size and high corporate reputation is not surprising. The remark of an English observer is relevant here: "The U.S. Public's perception of business is strongly in favor of large organizations. Public opinion polls confirm this time and time again. The average man in the street sees huge economic power as synonymous with the intelligence to use it wisely" (Thackray 1987: 69).

The industries where the price/earnings ratio was the most crucial variable and was more important than relative market share in relating to corporate reputation tended to be smaller in overall sales and to be composed of many smaller firms. These six industries were: metal manufacturing, diversified finance companies, commercial banking companies, retailing companies, transportation companies, and electronics and appliances.

Average yield was the most crucial variable for only one industry, food. Price/earnings ratio and average yield figures were not available for life insurance companies, therefore they were excluded from this analysis. For five industries—paper and fiber products, motor vehicles, metal products, life insurance, and diversified service companies—we could find no significant relationships between financial variables and overall corporate reputation. Their overall reputation was, however, importantly related to the relative size of the firm, with large firms having higher reputations.

Summary

The findings of Sobol and Farrelly are interesting in that they indicate that some major financial performance measures (earnings per share, price/earnings ratio, average yield, and net income) are quite important in perceptions of various aspects of corporate reputation. The extent of their importance, however, differs greatly across industries, as table 3.2 shows. Corporate reputations in the industries that have large-size firms tend to depend on the relative size of the corporation in its industry (market share), rather than actual measures of financial performance.

Even though the selected financial measures "explain" a good portion of the variability in corporate reputations, there is still unexplained variation. This leads to speculation regarding the other factors that may be important in assessing corporate reputations; characteristics such as age of the firm, lifecycle stages of products, reports in the managerial and/or financial press, and public relations activities may also prove to be crucial in assessing corporate reputation.

It may be possible to draw some meaningful comparisons between the concept of corporate reputation that is so important in management circles and the concept of risk that is so central to financial theoreticians and practitioners. The risk/return tradeoff observed in finance would seem to apply here, in that investing in high-reputation firms and being unwilling to accept risk implies a willingness to accept less return. The figures reported by Claire Makin (1983) support this, for in total return (price appreciation and dividend yield), the ten companies with the highest reputation failed to perform outstandingly well; their average annual ten-year median was 7.19 percent—lower than the ten-year median of 8.52 percent for the *Fortune* 500. Interestingly, a 1987 *Fortune* study (Baig 1987: 22) of companies with the lowest and highest reputation ratings in 1983 showed that net return (1982–1986) for the ten most admired companies was 16.445—only slightly higher than the 15.67 net return for the ten least admired firms. Thus, once firms have a high reputation, they may be in a position to offer lower current return to the investor because they offer a lower risk.

The McGuire–Sundgren–Schneeweis Study

Another important study on corporate reputation and financial issues by Jean B. McGuire, Alison Sundgren, and Thomas

Schneeweis (1988) explores the concept of corporate social responsibility, which has been very important in the recent concerns over oil spills, pollution, and pill tampering.

There are a number of theories about the relationship between a firm's social responsibility and its financial performance. One view (Aupperle, Carroll, and Hatfield 1985; Ullmann 1985; Vance 1975) holds that firms incur costs from socially responsible actions that put them at economic disadvantage compared to other less responsible firms. Diametrically opposed is the idea that the costs of social responsibility are small and therefore there are net benefits to the firm in terms of improved employee morale and productivity (Moskowitz 1972; Parket and Eibert 1975; Soloman and Hansen 1985). Still another view cited by McGuire, Sundgren, and Schneeweis says that costs of socially responsible action are large but they may be offset by other firm costs. For example, if stockholders, bondholders, and workers feel that product quality and social responsibility are poor they may doubt the firm's ability to honor its other claims and may demand higher dividends, interest rates, or wages. In addition, it has been suggested that stakeholders may see corporate social responsibility as indicating management skill (Alexander and Bucholtz 1978; Bowman and Haire 1975). Hence less responsible firms, lacking managerial skill, would be considered riskier investments and would find it more costly to raise needed funds.

The McGuire–Sundgren–Schneeweis study uses the *Fortune* ranking of social responsibility and relates social responsibility to prior and current financial performance using accounting as well as stock market-based measures to investigate the relationships among concurrently, previously, and subsequently measured firm performance and corporate social responsibility. Market performance was measured by risk-adjusted return (alpha) and total return; market risk measures were beta, which compares the risk of a particular firm to market risk, and the standard deviation of total return. Accounting-based performance measures were return on assets (ROA), total assets, sales growth, asset growth, and operating income growth. Accounting-based risk measures were ratio of debt to assets, operating leverage, and the standard deviation of operating income. Thus, a total of twelve variables were related to corporate responsibility. Corporate responsibility rankings for 1983–1985 were averaged for ninety-eight firms and corporate responsibility ratings from late 1982 (published in *Fortune* in January 1983) were related to financial performance variables for 1982–1984 and 1977–1981.

Concurrent performance relationships between social responsibility and stock market-based performance for the same period were insignificant. Three accounting based measures of performance did relate significantly to current corporate responsibility. These were return on assets and total assets, which showed a positive relationship, and operating income growth, which showed a negative relationship. The risk measures showed a negative relationship with corporate responsibility. Thus, we have a picture of the relatively large firms in terms of total assets (as in the Sobol–Farrelly study) showing the best corporate reputation for responsibility. This large firm size may also relate to the negative relationship of growth and good reputation as large well-established firms growing at a slower rate also are probably considered to have less risk than less established firms.

When McGuire et al. related prior firm performance to social responsibility the stock market measures are not correlated; the accounting-based performance measures ROA, sales growth, and asset growth, however, are significantly associated with a high level of social responsibility. The authors suggest that "low risk firms and firms with a high return on assets will later have an image of high social responsibility" (p. 865). This may arise from the fact that these firms have the financial capacity to expend resources on social responsibility tasks rather than that the management is so capable. Of course, it may be that a capable manager can keep firm risk low and ROA high!

When relationships between corporate social responsibility and performance measured at a later time are studied, return on assets (ROA) is again highly correlated with social responsibility. Both stock market- and accounting-based risk measures were negatively related to previous social responsibility. Overall accounting-based performance measures had a higher explanatory value than stock market performance. The authors suggest that "one possible reason for these results is that the two market-based measures, total return and beta are related primarily to systematic movements among all firms. In contrast, accounting measures are more likely to capture unique, or unsystematic firm attributes" (p. 868). Since actions leading to high or low perceived corporate social responsibility may be predominately unsystematic, accounting performance may be more likely to show a relationship to social responsibility. Thus in summary, high prior performance and low prior risk were better predictors of high corporate responsibility ratings than were concurrent or subsequent accounting and stock market performance and risk. Firms that had done well could afford to exhibit social responsibility. Furthermore, accounting measures were better related to responsibility than were stock market measures. The authors suggest that some outcomes of their results are that it seems that financial performance influences social responsibility. Second, they suggest that reduction of firm risk is an important benefit of social responsibility and this has been overlooked in most previous studies.

The *Fortune* articles and the McGuire–Sundgren–Schneeweis study all presume that a reputation for social responsibility is an asset for the firm. A controversial article by Alfred Rappaport in the *New York Times* points out that "the only social responsibility of business is to create shareholder wealth and to do so legally and with integrity" (1990: F13). He feels that corporate management lacks the political legitimacy and expertise to decide what is in the social interest. This decision he feels should be made by elected legislators and the judicial system. An active market for takeovers, according to Rappaport, shows little tolerance for management that is not attentive to shareholder value. Business decisions based on social rather than economic criteria may trigger the corrective mechanisms of takeovers and restructuring. Moreover, investments in socially responsible expenditures that do not increase the value of the company or its stock will be passed on to consumers by way of higher prices, or to employees as lower wages, or to shareholders as lower returns.

The picture of whether the impression that a firm is socially responsible leads to higher profits or market value is not clear. According to McGuire et al., prior high profits and low risk were better predictors of high corporate responsibility ratings than were subsequent performance and risk. Thus, firms doing well by accounting and stock market measures are most likely to expend money at some later date on social responsibilities. Subsequent accounting and risk performance may not be a result of high corporate reputation. Similarly, Sobol and Farrelly found that generally there was a positive relation (see table 3.2) between previous financial measures (PE 1976, AY 1981, PE 1981, PE 1973, and AY 1977) and social responsibility ratings for 1982. In only one case (PE 1977) was there a negative relation between previous financial measures and views of the corporate responsibility of the firm. Thus, when a firm is doing well, it seems to provide funds for social responsibility. It is still not clear whether a good reputation for corporate responsibility leads to extra profitability. This may be a curvilinear relationship where some evidence of good corporate responsibility enhances corporate profits, but where extremely high investment in corporate responsibility expenditures detracts from the net profitability of the firm. Thus, the firm may have to deal with efforts to satisfy stockholder demands and the financing of corporate responsibility objectives. Certainly, the criteria for this balance is an important area for future research.

STUDIES THAT DO NOT USE THE *FORTUNE* REPUTATION RATINGS

The articles discussed up to this point have related financial variables to the *Fortune* reputation rankings. In this next section, we review articles which look at some of the aspects covered by the *Fortune* corporate reputation rankings such as ability to attract and keep good employees, quality of management and quality of product. These articles do not use the *Fortune* rankings but they discuss research on issues covered by the rankings in the areas *Fortune* rated.

Ability to Attract and Keep People

In the previous section we discussed the relationship between one aspect of corporate reputation (corporate responsibility) and financial factors. Another aspect of reputation in the *Fortune* survey is ability to attract and keep people. There are non-pecuniary attractions that employers can offer (Schwoerer and Rosen 1989). Prime among these are *job security*. Some firms may offer corporate due process where discharge can be only "for cause" while other firms use employment-at-will policies that permit termination of employees for just cause, no cause, or even bad cause at any time (Leonard 1983). Sometimes employment policy may interact with compensation policies so that workers are willing to forego some amount of job security in return for extra compensation.

A recent study by Catherine Schwoerer and Benson Rosen (1989: 655) indicates that "the statement of employment-at-will policy significantly lowers evaluation of the company as a prospective employer." Another finding was that high compensation could offset employment-at-will policies in terms of students' job pursuit intentions.

Thus, firms face cost tradeoffs in regard to reputation. Higher wages may offset ability to lay off at will in terms of workers' willingness to consider a job with a company. In terms of corporate reputation, it would seem that the firm with due process had a higher reputation. For many years IBM pursued a policy of a lifetime job guarantee and for many years IBM's corporate reputation was in the top ten in the *Fortune* studies. As indicated in chapter 2, however, IBM has not been in the top ten in the last four surveys. At the same time, the lifetime job guarantee at IBM has become weaker and weaker. It is interesting to reflect on whether there is a causal relationship between the two factors, and if so, in which "direction" the causality runs. It is the typical chicken-and-egg dilemma. Does a lifetime job guarantee lead to overstaffing, poor financial performance, and a lower reputation? Or does a lower reputation and poor financial performance "cause" a firm to lessen the strength of its lifetime job guarantee?

Quality of Management

Another of the eight factors thought to have an important influence on corporate reputation is quality of management. Quality of management may involve a number of behavioral activities performed by managers. In a recent article, Anne S. Tsui (1984) studied forty activities and classified them using factor analyses into six major managerial roles. The six roles were leader, spokesperson, resource allocator, entrepreneur, environment monitor, and liaison. The activities in each of the groups are described in table 3.3 (1984: 72–73).

In this research, the managers who met behavioral expectations were adjudged to have good managerial reputations. The managers were evaluated by three constituencies: (1) superiors who might emphasize the entrepreneurial role; (2) subordinates who might emphasize the leader, resource allocator, and environment monitor roles; and (3) peers who might emphasize the spokesperson and liaison roles.

To be judged effective, a manager must be rated above the median by all three types of evaluators. Actually, only 11 percent of the 217 managers (24) were judged to be reputationally effective by all three constituencies. Thirteen percent (28) of the managers were ranked as poor by all three constituencies. A third category of 47 percent (101) were ranked as partially reputationally effective. The remaining 64 were unclassified due to missing responses from either one or more constituencies. The high-, partial-, and low-reputation managers were then studied

Table 3.3
Managerial Duties for Six Managerial Roles

Leader

    Evaluate quality of subordinates' job performance
    Integrate subordinates' goals with company requirements
    Forward important work information to subordinates
    Direct work of subordinates
    Allocate human resources to tasks
    Resolve conflicts between subordinates
    Facilitate subordinates' growth and development
    Give negative feedback
    Alert subordinates to problems
    Use authority to ensure subordinates complete tasks
    Provide new employees with training

Spokesperson

    Serve as expert to people outside unit
    Keep others informed of unit's future plans
    Answer inquiries about unit
    Serve on committees, represent unit
    Provide information to others about unit's activities

Resource Allocator

    Distribute budgeted resources
    Make decisions about time parameters
    Prevent loss of human or capital resources
    Allocate monies within unit
    Decide which programs to provide resources
    Allocate equipment or materials

Enterpreneur

    Plan and implement changes
    Initiate controlled changes
    Solve problems by instituting needed changes

Environment Monitor

    Initiate new ideas for business or operation
    Keep up with market trends
    Keep up with company's operational progress
    Keep up with technological development
    Scan environment for opportunities
    Gather information about customers and competitors
    Tour facilities for observational purposes
    Learn about new ideas from outside units
    Read reports about own or other units

Liaison

    Attend social functions to keep up contacts
    Attend meetings in other units
    Stay attuned to informal network
    Develop or maintain contacts by answering inquiries
    Develop contacts with important outside people

Source: Table 1, Tsui, Anne S. "A Role Set Analysis of Managerial
         Reputation," Organizational Behavior and Human Performance,
         Vol. 34 (1984) pp. 72-73.

according to their performance appraisal in the company based on four company success factors. These were performance appraisal rating, merit increase (percent of base salary), intracompany promotion rate, and career advancement rate. In all cases the managers who had been ranked highest by peers, subordinates, and superiors ranked highest in terms of these four managerial success criteria. Also, it was clear that the expectations for different desirable managerial behaviors varied by the status of the evaluator. Thus, as stated before the roles leading to high rankings by subordinates were those of leader, resource allocator, and environment monitor, while superiors valued entrepreneurship and peers valued the spokesperson and liaison roles.

How does this relate to the *Fortune* study of reputation for managerial effectiveness? As we can see, managerial effectiveness evaluation criteria seem to vary by the role of the evaluator. Is the evaluator a peer, a subordinate, or a superior? *Fortune* mails its survey questionnaires to senior executives, outside directors, and financial analysts. So, for the most part (with the possible exception of financial analysts), the survey is sent to peers. Indeed, in our survey section in the next chapter where we interviewed CEOs and ex-CEOs, we encountered a number of people who said that they had filled out the *Fortune* corporate reputation survey many times. Thus, many of these evaluators would have the rank of peer or possibly superior. We may, therefore, be able to assume that as peers they were primarily looking at the spokesperson and liaison roles of the managers as sources of high or low corporate reputation. This stresses the crucial importance of liaison and communication and public relations activities in enhancing the managerial reputation of the firm. If we also assume that those ranking corporate reputation for quality of management are CEOs and are looking at the firm from the standpoint of superiors, then the importance of entrepreneurship is also crucial. As we can see from table 3.3, the crucial duties here are to plan and implement changes. Thus, as Stan Sauerhoft and Chris Atkins (1989) point out, today's companies have no place to hide. Activists, gadflies, legislators, and regulators scrutinize companies more closely than ever before. These opinions also depend on the evaluators' vested interests. Investors evaluate good earnings while environmentalists may think only of how the company facilities affect the air and water in the community. The authors suggest that the corporate image is a huge mosaic and effective communication aimed at various "stakeholders"—employees, customers, unions, community government, and others—will pay off when a crisis occurs.

Quality of Product

Classical market economics has assumed that a consumer can evaluate product quality soon after purchase and that all other consumers will hear of this evaluation soon after it is made. Thus, in the long run, there will be no misrepresentation of quality by firms. As a result, according to William P. Rogerson (1983: 508), who uses a theoretical economic proof, high-quality firms have more customers because they have fewer dissatisfied customers who leave and word of mouth advertising results in more arrivals. Second, higher fixed costs are usually associated with better quality and these costs may form barriers to entry of new firms. Thus, the high-quality firms may tend to be the larger firms. This finding correlates well with the Sobol–Farrelly empirical results showing that the firms with larger market share in their industry tend to be the firms with highest overall reputations.

Rogerson goes on to point out that there are problems in the way information on product quality is communicated from one consumer to another. Consumers are generally unable to transmit objective descriptions or product or firm performance; firms consequently rely on such issues as to whether the consumer will or will not purchase from the firm again. Policies that enable objective quality data to be exchanged, such as government activity to establish a consumer metric (Beales, Croswell, and Salop 1981), might develop a common language to describe products and, hence, make quality of the product a more measurable item. Private, not-for-profit organizations that engage in product evaluation such as the Consumer's Union, which annually evaluates a wide variety of products and services, can also be very helpful in aiding consumer choice and according reputation for outstanding product quality to deserving companies.

In another theoretical article, Carl Shapiro (1982) has analyzed monopoly behavior when consumers cannot evaluate all relevant attributes of a product prior to purchase. In general, the proof shows that the optimal quality the firm chooses to produce is lower than it would be in a perfect information setting. The result applies both in the case of a once-and-for-all quality choice and in the case of quality choice over time. Possibly it could be inferred from this study that in an industry where one firm has a very large market share, quality reputation may represent quality that is not as high as it is reputed to be. The link between what it is profitable for a firm to do and what a firm actually does, however, has not been made. Moreover, there are very few actual monopoly situations in any product market so that competition may force firms to maintain reasonably good quality of their product.

CONCLUDING REMARKS ABOUT THE ACADEMIC LITERATURE

In general, the academic literature does seem to show some connection between financial variables and corporate reputation; but this connection appears to be tenuous at best. Apparently, there are a host of factors (some financial and some nonfinancial) that determine corporate reputation. And most likely, the same set of factors does not perform exactly the same from one firm to another. This suggests that we need to do a lot more research on the topic of corporate reputation.

Walter P. Margulies, in an article in *Management Review* (1979: 16), states that "the ability to raise needed capital depends largely on how investors perceive and value the business." He goes on to point out that public relations activity may be very valuable in raising the price/earnings ratio. Thus, in the next chapter, we report on our survey of public relations specialists; their views on corporate reputation are important. Through a comprehensive public relations plan, executives can exercise significant control over investor perceptions and evaluations of their firms.

NOTES

1. The authors are grateful to *Fortune* and the Erdos and Morgan Research Service for sharing this data.

2. R^2, the coefficient of determination, shows what percent of variation in reputation is explained by this variable. Generally, it is difficult to explain 100 percent of behavior, so a total R^2 of .38 can be considered very important if a large enough sample is used. Stepwise multiple regression in the Statistical Package for the Social Sciences (Nie et al. 1975) computer program was used to analyze the data.

CHAPTER 4

Survey of PR Practitioners and Specialists

We have examined some academic studies on corporate reputation as well as the *Fortune* studies on this important topic. There is, however, much more left to be explained; no one knows exactly how and why corporate reputations are either improved or destroyed. To get more information, therefore, we turned to experts in the corporate reputation field—public relations specialists. Their views, we reasoned, are crucially important. To a certain extent, these are the people who mold public perceptions of corporate reputation.

An in-depth survey of public relations practitioners (employed in corporate firms) and public relations specialists (consultants) was an integral part of this study of corporate reputation. We were interested in a number of issues about corporate reputation, including the following:

- Where do they get information about corporate reputation?
- What are the most important audiences for corporate reputation programs?

- What are the key elements in developing a PR plan and who is involved in the process?
- What is the influence of corporate reputation on employee recruitment and retention, financial management, sales, and community relations?
- How do they rank the eight *Fortune* attributes of corporate reputation?
- How have public relations programs changed over the years?
- What are the important issues of the 1990s?

Questionnaires were sent to a select sample of public relations practitioners in various industries, ranging from consumer goods to manufacturing to medical services. In addition, representatives of PR agencies that employed from 2 to 2,300 persons were contacted. We found quite a bit of agreement and a number of very original and creative ideas in the answers to these surveys. In this chapter, we will analyze the findings of our study. We will also interweave these findings with suggestions for handling PR plans, important issues for the future, and potential economic benefits that a good corporate reputation can give a company.

To establish a frame of reference for our survey, first we asked participants to define corporate reputation. In general everyone agreed that corporate reputation is the way a corporation is perceived by its various audiences (also referred to as "publics"). On a more personal level, it was defined as "my gut reaction about a company" and "the first five words that come to my mind about a company." The public relations professionals were also quick to point out that each company's reputation was different, depending on their audiences' experiences. Corporate reputation then is not a single monolithic opinion, but rather the synthesis of a variety of considered opinions about operations, image, quality, customer service, community involvement, employee relations, management style, financial strength, and use of corporate assets.

Just as important as what corporate reputation is defined as, we felt it was necessary to determine what benefits a company can derive from a "good" corporate reputation and what the consequences of a "bad" corporate reputation are. One of our participants, Cynthia Pharr, president and CEO of Tracy–Locke/Pharr Public Relations, summarized the sentiments of most of the participants. "A good corporate reputation can help a company by earning it extra consideration, and extra goodwill. These both can have a tangible effect on the company as consumers may have more willingness to try a new product and they also may offer more forgiveness of mistakes." The public relations professionals felt strongly that good corporate reputation provided support during a crisis, loyalty from employees, extra valuation from financial markets, and credibility in new product or service endeavors. A manager of a local office of a national advertising and PR firm added that "Good corporate reputation creates a halo effect around that company's products or services that can enhance sales and share price."

While "good" corporate reputation appears to add to the bottom line, those surveyed believe even more strongly that "bad" corporate reputation detracts from it. Overall those surveyed felt a "bad" corporate reputation would reduce business and cause customers to seek alternatives. Bad reputation also contributed to creating poor morale for employees and to reducing the number and strength of investors. "If a company has a bad reputation people give it no breaks or any extra consideration. They believe the worst and sell their stock if they hear a rumor, abandon the products if there is a quality problem and some people will quit their jobs so as not to be associated with a bad company," said Pharr. A public relations professional with a large national telecommunications firm put the consequences on an even broader scale by noting that a "bad" corporate reputation can make companies the target of activist group and terrorists. While a "good" corporate reputation will enhance the business effort, survey participants felt a "bad" corporate reputation could put a company out of business.

GETTING FEEDBACK ON REPUTATION STATUS

How do PR people get information on the reputations of their clients? The chief methods cited by the PR specialists are listed below:

1. Research on media comments and coverage comments of reporters and analysts.
2. Comments of customer focus groups and results of customer surveys.
3. Customer service complaints and comments. "Word of mouth" was the most frequently advised method. To us, this was an especially interesting finding. Here we are in the modern age, characterized by all sorts of fancy mechanisms for communication. But computers, fax machines, and other kinds of electronic gadgets can never replace the plain old basic human mouth. "Word of mouth" might include:
   a. Talking to community members, particularly leaders in the local community.
   b. Talking to employees.
   c. Talking to business associates.
   d. Talking to competitors.
   e. Talking to financial people such as stockbrokers.

Finally, many PR directors mentioned "personal experience." They defined personal experience as personally purchasing and using a product. This seems to be an admission that what counts most in determining reputation are facts rather than perceptions!

PUBLIC RELATIONS PLANS

Planning is a crucial part of all business. Most companies have sales and marketing plans, product development plans, long–

range strategic plans, and a variety of other plans to help them define the bottom line. Companies should also develop PR plans. When PR specialists were surveyed, four out of five said their corporate clients developed an annual PR plan. Public relations plans serve as guidelines showing how a corporation will carry out all of its public relations efforts. Oftentimes these plans are developed in a crisis situation as responsive plans of action. Companies can get more mileage out of "proactive" plans that are designed to communicate their message. Developing these plans allows companies to control the message they communicate to their audiences. Such plans can be developed and implemented at leisure, rather than in the harsh glare of the public spotlight turned on by a crisis.

The issue of reactive versus proactive strategy is an especially important one and relates in some sense to the entire business, not just to the PR plan. In fact, according to Michel M. Robert (1990: 24–28), the lack of proactive strategy may be the main reason that in the last ten to fifteen years American multinationals have lost ground to Japanese and German companies. Corporate America is engrossed in techniques and formulas of competitive strategy. But, according to Robert (p. 24), "a strategy developed entirely on competitive analysis will always be, by its very nature, a reactive strategy and not a proactive one." Robert cites the example of Akio Morita, founder of Sony, who had no competitive data when the decision to introduce the videocassette recorder or the Walkman was made. According to Robert (p. 24), "strategy based on competitive analysis may only make the organization overlook other lucrative opportunities outside its existing competitive arena. . . . Competition is indeed a variable in the strategic process, but it is not the first variable to consider, nor is it the most important." Companies that stick to reactive strategies are permitting themselves to be led. In following the pack, they will probably achieve only mediocre performance. On the other hand, those with proactive strategies that are successful will probably be rewarded with excellent results in recognition of their leadership role.

Public relations plans should address a wide range of areas. In developing PR plans, it should be remembered that the plans will not work overnight or even in just one year. These plans should be developed with long-term goals and immediate and short-term action steps. A PR plan that is developed and stored on a shelf or in a manual is a wasted effort. Once these plans are established they should become working documents that are revised to meet the changing needs of customers and environments. How often they are revised should be determined by the committee that develops them. Oftentimes companies leave out the element of evaluation when such plans are developed. This is a key step and many times it is the most valuable part of the plan. If employees know they will be evaluated on their PR efforts they are more likely to set and meet measurable goals.

Who is involved in developing this annual PR plan? Answers to this question covered a wide range of possibilities. In some companies the only participants were the entire PR department. Most companies extended the planning process. For example, one large telecommunications company included the PR department, working with marketing and senior management. In other companies, the groups involved were extended vertically within the company. They included top executives, marketing, public affairs and communications executives, and managers—as well as managers of operational units. Others extended upward and nationally, including PR department and executive management and headquarters PR department (in another state). This company did not include managers of operational units.

Certainly it seems to be a good idea to include operational units, especially for crucial new products. Inclusion of, or at least consultation with, national headquarters is also a good idea since national campaigns should correlate with and aid the local branch's public relations efforts. The practitioners and specialists all agreed that top management must buy into the plans for them to be effective.

What are the key elements in developing a PR plan? Every corporation will have a different approach to developing a public relations plan. Some have committees that meet annually; some hire outside consultants; some do not develop a plan; and others meet on a monthly basis to update plans. The only thing that is consistent in developing and carrying out these plans is that there is no consistency in how they are developed and implemented.

Although this was an open-ended question in our survey of public relations specialists, the answers about key elements in developing a PR plan fell into several easily distinguishable categories. Since these may be useful as "what to do guides," we have listed the categories and types of actions in table 4.1. The first section involves knowledge, research, and analysis. Before developing an annual PR plan, one should know and understand the business plan of the entire firm. In addition, one should know the specific goals of the regional or branch office for whom the plan is being developed if it is not done on a national scope. Input from various departments such as marketing is highly desirable.

As we can see in table 4.1, it is crucial to understand the audience for the public relations activities. The third step is to decide on PR goals and strategies and to prioritize these strategies. A fourth step is to determine a budget and other resources for the PR plan. Given the priorities, one will probably have to decide how far one can proceed in each of the areas specified for the plan.

The next step is to be sure the projects are simple, workable, and measurable. To do this, one may have to change the plans several times and reiterate some of the earlier steps to make sure the plan is still accomplishing the desired goals. Companies should also ensure that their plan is creative and forward-thinking. Table 4.1 indicates some questions the company might ask itself as it forms its PR plan.

The plan should then be communicated to top management and to the "rank and file." Once again, this may lead to more revisions. Because of these revisions, the development of the annual PR plan may take considerable time. Constant review will help to ensure that the PR time and funds are well spent.

Table 4.1
How to Develop an Annual PR Plan

I. Research and Analysis	1.	Know the Business Plan.
	2.	Understand the Business Plan.
	3.	Get input from the Marketing Department.
	4.	Understand the Business Environment.
	5.	Know company goals and those of your particular location.
II. Identify and Understand Audiences	1.	Who is the audience?
	2.	What are their wants and needs?
	3.	What are their goals?
III. Decide on and Prioritize Goals and Strategies	1.	What are they?
	2.	Are they adequate?
IV. Determine a Budget for Your PR Plan	1.	Who are your key resources?
	2.	How much money do you need to carry out your plan?
V. Make Project Simple Workable, Measurable	1.	Design your message to be in line with the business plan.
	2.	Set realistic expectations.
	3.	Do clients understand what you intend to do?
VI. Be Innovative and Forward Thinking	1.	Know where you are headed.
	2.	What are the trends in your particular industry?
	3.	What can we do differently?
	4.	How will we adapt to change?
VII. Develop Plan to Communicate the PR Plan	1.	Be sure plan is communicated to top management.
	2.	Be sure to communicate the plan to rank and file.

Table 4.1 (Continued)

VIII. Implement the Plan	1.	Determine who will carry out each part of the plan.
	2.	Set target start dates and deadlines for implementing specific steps.
	3.	Monitor the progress of the steps.
	4.	Communicate the progress of the implementation.
IX. Evaluate the Results	1.	Once the plans have been completed, evaluate the results on the following questions:
		- Did they meet your original goals?
		- Does the plan need to be modified for next year?
		- Were the right people assigned to the right tasks?
		- Are there other areas that need to be addressed by the plans?
		- How has your client base reacted to the effort?
		- How have your employees reacted to the effort?
		- What worked well in the plans?
		- What can be done to improve the plans?

Finally, the most crucial parts of the planning process are the implementation and evaluation phases. As stated previously in this chapter, these plans must become working documents. People should be assigned specific tasks and held accountable for their completion. A monitoring system should be put into place. It may be discovered during the implementation phases that some of the plans need to be adapted to meet changing needs and environments. These changes can be addressed in the evaluation process. The evaluation phase can begin as soon as

Table 4.2
PR Specialists' Rankings of Corporate Reputation Attributes*

		Average Rank
1.	Quality of Products and Services	1.5
2.	Quality of Management	2.5
3.	Financial Soundness	3.7
4.	Ability to Attract and Keep Talented People	3.8
5.	Innovativeness	4.8
6.	Long Term Investment Value	5.4
7.	Community and Environmental Responsibility	6.4
8.	Use of Corporate Assets	7.5

*These are the eight attributes covered in the Fortune reputation surveys.

the first deadline has passed. Table 4.1 lists several questions that should be addressed in the ongoing evaluation process. In our survey the PR specialists pointed out that the evaluation phase is often left out. It must not be neglected, however, if the plans are expected to be effective.

RANKING THE IMPORTANCE OF THE *FORTUNE* SURVEY REPUTATION ATTRIBUTES

As part of our survey of PR practitioners and consultants, we asked them to rank the eight criteria for good reputation used in the *Fortune* studies. The results are shown in table 4.2. We have listed the criteria in terms of their importance to our respondents with the top ones first.

These criteria were ranked from 1 to 8, with 1 being the highest ranking. The ranks shown here are averages of the rankings given by the respondents. It comes through "loud and clear" that quality of products and services (1.5) is most important. Second, we have quality of management (2.5), third are financial soundness

(3.7) and ability to attract and keep talented people (3.8). These results are slightly different than the responses to the *Fortune* survey. As mentioned in chapter 2, in that survey, quality of management is consistently ranked first and quality of products or services second. In the report of the latest *Fortune* survey, however, the second choice (quality of products or services) is narrowing the gap. If this trend were to continue, perhaps the two attributes will eventually switch places, with quality of products and services being perceived as the most important attribute of corporate reputation.

WHAT CAN A GOOD REPUTATION DO FOR A COMPANY?

There are several areas where a good reputation can help a company. These are categorized in table 4.3. In the labor market one may be able to hire better workers for lower salaries (Tsui 1984; Schwoerer and Rosen 1989). Financing may be easier for the company with a good image. Product sales may be facilitated and may require less advertising. Community relationships may be easier and zoning and "tax breaks" may be more accessible for the "good company." In our survey of PR practitioners and PR consultants we asked them to rate a number of possibilities in these four areas on a scale from 1 (utmost importance) to 5 (not important). Table 4.3 shows the averages of their ratings.

There were three areas in the labor field where the PR consultants and practitioners thought a good reputation would help: attracting a better quality of worker, increasing employee loyalty, and providing a larger selection of potential employees. While these areas are important benefits of good corporate reputation, having a good corporate reputation will not allow a company to lower wages or benefits.

In the financial area good reputation improves ability to sell more stock and to float more loans. It is not as likely to lower

Table 4.3
PR Specialists' Ratings of What a Good Corporate Image Can Do for a Company

	Average Ratings
Labor	
Larger selection of potential employees	2.1
Better quality of workers	1.2
Increased employee loyalty	2.0
Lower wage rates possible	4.4
Less expensive benefit plans possible	4.1
Finance	
Ability to float more loans	2.2
Lower interest rate on loans	3.1
Less restriction on selling bonds	4.1
Ability to issue stock at higher prices	3.0
Ability to sell more stock	1.9
Product/Service Sales	
Ability to sell high quantities	2.7
Ability to charge higher prices	2.2
Ability to devote less $ to advertising	4.1
Ability to expand product line	2.7
Ability to sell through more dealers	2.5
Community	
Ability to locate in better communities	4.2
Increased possibility for business extensions	2.4
Ability to deal with local governments	2.9
Ability to obtain media coverage	3.0
Ability to establish consumer trust	1.4

The highest rating is 1 (utmost importance) and the lowest rating is 5 (not important).

interest rates on loans or to allow for the issue of stock at higher prices, however.

In the product/service sales area a good reputation, however, enables the firm to sell products or services at higher prices. It also enables the firm to sell through many dealers, to expand product lines, and to sell high quantities. It does not help a company to spend less on advertising.

With respect to the community the most important result of a good reputation is establishment of consumer trust. A good reputation would help a firm extend business, deal with local governments, and obtain more media coverage. The least important advantage is the ability to locate in better communities.

There are a wide variety of benefits from a good reputation. Fourteen factors were rated between 1 and 3, which means that the PR specialists considered them important.

CHANGES IN PR PLANS OVER THE YEARS

When the PR specialists and PR professionals were questioned about how PR plans had changed over the last decade a number of areas of agreement were perceived. First, there is more management involvement. This has had a number of consequences. The PR people have gained a better understanding of the businesses they serve. Often PR personnel participate in helping firms to make strategic decisions. One PR professional noted that over the years, the department expanded and took on many new responsibilities, including meeting planning, executive communications, and international marketing. Because of this increasing use of PR services some felt that there was a widening gap between CEOs who understand the value of communications and those who do not. Michel M. Robert's *The Strategist CEO: How Visionary Executives Build Organizations* (1989) contains much valuable advice for CEOs who really understand the value of communication. A second area that has changed is the use of the new electronic media. These include fax, voice mail, and video news releases.

The PR personnel also felt that the newer PR programs are more focused. They are not aimed solely at good will. Instead they strive for multiple goals, with emphasis on measurable results. This is in keeping with the increased emphasis of business in general on quantitative rather than merely qualitative analysis of efforts and results. They are more specialized and often represent intensified support of sales. Thus PR is more market-driven than it was a decade ago.

CORPORATE REPUTATION ISSUES FOR THE 1990s

While a number of issues that will affect corporations and their reputations in the 1990s were suggested, several appeared over and over in our surveys of the public relations professionals:

- Quality products and services
- Global competition
- Qualified employee recruiting
- Environmental responsibility
- Cost consciousness

Quality products and services will continue to be a driving force in the quest for corporate reputation. Without quality products and services companies cannot expect to achieve or maintain a "good" reputation. Consumers rely on companies to produce quality products and to provide excellent services. Consumers continually seek products and services that are convenient to use. The prestige of the Malcolm Baldrige National Quality Awards is well known throughout the United States. Companies that have won the awards think of them as valuable assets and make use of them in advertising. According to Gilbert Fuchsberg (1991: B5), "Supporters of the award maintain it has greatly boosted quality awareness and a competitive spirit in many companies." The Baldrige Awards are discussed more fully in Chapter 6.

There will be more global competitors, such as Japan and the third world countries. More competition is also expected from European and other markets. Companies will be expected to increase their ability to communicate internationally and to design products for international markets.

Environmental responsibility has become and will continue to be a major concern for the 1990s. Corporations are being held responsible by their publics for environmental issues. The public wants to deal with companies that care about the environment and have jumped on the bandwagon to help make this planet a better place to live in the future. As Americans become more "environmentally" aware, corporations will not only have to initiate and continue programs to save the environment, but also communicate their efforts to their audiences. According to Craig Smith, editor and publisher of the *Corporate Philanthropy Report* (1990: F11), "Philanthropy is also a marketing issue. In most mature industries, there are a number of products of the same quality and price. When you have that circumstance, corporate citizenship makes the critical difference between whether a company's product can be trusted or not. A recent Roper poll showed that 52 percent of consumers said they will pay more for a socially responsible product. Companies viewed as socially responsible have a marketing edge."

The shrinking labor pool of the future has become a major issue. Corporations will have to concentrate on their reputation (especially in dealing with employee relations) to continue to be able to recruit and retain qualified employees.

With the start of the 1990s showing the economy in a recession, consumers are more cost-conscious. Corporations will have to emphasize their concern with the economy and prove that they can produce a value-added product. They must minimize cost and yet maximize the value of their products.

In Chapter 5, we will ask many of the same questions of CEOs and compare their answers to those of the public relations specialists. In addition, we shall study the popular business literature to see how the CEOs view the different attributes of reputation and to see what they advise other companies to do in these areas. In the remaining chapters of this book, we offer some suggestions (backed by examples of specific actions taken by actual firms) for dealing with the five issues mentioned above, as well as numerous other challenges which may arise in the next decade. These chapters should serve as food for thought for those facing the challenge of building corporate reputations in the 1990s and beyond.

CHAPTER 5

Opinions of the CEO

According to James G. Gray, Jr. (1986:72), the chief executive officer is a crucial factor in the establishment of corporate image.

Corporate identity has come to rest on the shoulders of the chief executive officer and other top-rung managers. . . . The chief executive officer is the voice of the corporation, a voice that reflects the image of the entire organization.

In the role of corporate spokesperson, the chief executive officer assumes the burden of defining, molding and communicating the corporate view. Part of the task is to assure that corporate policies are expressed in a way that reflects the corporation as a credible, open entity responsive to public expectations.

Noting the importance of the CEO, we decided to search the literature and interview several CEOs to find their views of corporate reputation. In our in-depth discussions, we primarily talked to CEOs of large firms similar to those covered in the *Fortune* reputation studies; we did, however, include CEOs of some smaller firms. The interviews posed the same questions to the CEOs as those asked of the public relations specialists and the public relations practitioners. In this chapter, we shall compare the answers of the CEOs and the public relations people and we shall look at the view of CEOs as interviewed in this study and from interviews in popular business publications. We shall cover the following issues:

- Where do they get information about corporate reputation?
- What are the most important audiences for corporate reputation programs?
- What are key things a company can do to enhance reputation?
- What are their rankings of the eight *Fortune* attributes of corporate reputation?
- What is the influence of corporate reputation on labor, finance, sales, and community?

GETTING FEEDBACK ON REPUTATION STATUS

Personal experience seemed to be the most important method for CEOs to get information about their reputation. Many, as recommended by Peter Drucker, manage by "walking around outside." For example, Al Casey, former CEO of American Airlines, said that he would usually "do one airplane trip per day." Another CEO of a lumber company said he would talk to competitors to see how his company would "stack up" in the industry. A CEO of a smaller sales company mentioned other people in the same industry as sources of information on his company.

The second most commonly mentioned source of information on reputation for CEOs, especially for the publicly held companies, was the reports of market analysts like Shearson, Goldman Sachs, and Eppley–Guerin. The CEOs felt that these analysts really understood their businesses. Most analysts work in specialized fields and eventually have a good "feel" for the specific industries that they study.

The CEOs also received "word of mouth" feedback from customers and employees. Some felt that the problem with customer feedback was that generally they heard from customers only when products were deficient.

Richard Haayen, former CEO of Allstate, stated in a recent interview that he used research studies of policyholders to see what the company reputation was and how the company could give customers better service.

The CEOs, however, did not use as much research on media coverage as the PR people did nor did they mention focus groups. Thus, the PR people might do more to enlighten CEOs on the possibilities of content analysis and media research in assessing reputation. On the other hand, another method of evaluating reputation used by the CEOs that was not mentioned by the PR people was objective measures such as "time to pay off on claims" or on-time performance of airplane departures and arrivals. One problem with this method of evaluation is that the CEO may be aware of the excellent objective performance of the company but the customers may not know of this excellent record! In a recent article on "Championing Change," Raymond Smith, the CEO of Bell Atlantic who is noted for transforming a monopolistic bureaucratic corporation into one that is both efficient and entrepreneurial, lists the twelve obligations of leadership for Bell Atlantic executives. The fifth obligation reads as follows: "Obtain the necessary information to communicate Bell Atlantic's values, mission, goals, strategies and corporate positions to all of our constituents" (Kanter 1991: 121). So the firm needs to communicate to the public, and the CEO should work together with the PR personnel to let the publics know about the firm. If the company has a record for "on-time" performance, advertise it!

WHAT ARE THE IMPORTANT AUDIENCES FOR CORPORATE REPUTATION PROGRAMS?

When this question was posed to the CEOs, there was some divergence of answers. Most felt that the customers were the most important, others pointed to employees, and others mentioned stockholders. No one selected creditors or security analysts.

WHAT ARE THREE KEY THINGS A COMPANY CAN DO TO ENHANCE ITS CORPORATE REPUTATION?

One executive said, "service, service, service—serve your customers." Stan Rabin, CEO of Commercial Metals, offered the following trio: credibility, integrity, and reliability. A third CEO replied, "Perform as promised (good quality) and happy employees—*awareness* of employee problems." Once again, we see a divergence of CEO views. Quality of the product and reliability do, however, emerge as important bases for good reputation.

According to Rod Canion, former CEO of Compaq Computers, quality has an all–pervasive definition. He says (Webber 1990: 121–122), "Quality isn't whether or not your products work. Quality is how people do their job. Quality is defining your job and then meeting the expectations. When you do that, you raise everyone's consciousness that everything is important. Every piece of the company is important."

With regard to credibility, Canion makes the following comments in the same article:

To be a leader you have to do more than just get out in front. A lot of small companies go for the headlines by announcing a product first. That works to get headlines, but it doesn't work well to get sales because you have to combine being first to the market with having credibility with customers so that they'll follow you. Leadership is about not being held back by your competition and also having *credibility* and clout with customers so they'll go with you." (p. 123)

RANKING THE IMPORTANCE OF THE *FORTUNE* SURVEY REPUTATION ATTRIBUTES

We asked CEOs to rank the eight criteria for good reputation used in the *Fortune* studies. The average results are shown in table

5.1, where we have also shown PR specialists' and practitioners' ratings. These criteria were ranked from 1 to 8, with 1 being the highest ranking. Quality of products and services is most important to both groups. PR people scored it 1.5 and CEOs scored it 1.75.

Surprisingly, the second most important ranking by the CEOs was accorded to innovativeness (2.8); this quality was rated in fifth place by the PR specialists and professionals. Tsui (1984) pointed out that superiors might evaluate managers in terms of innovativeness. Thus, to the CEO who evaluates another company, performance might relate to personal ideas of what managers should do. As Tsui pointed out, the entrepreneur's function includes planning and implementing changes, initiating controlled changes, and solving problems by instituting needed changes. Certainly, the recent literature in the popular business journals has stressed innovativeness.

Professor Andrall E. Pearson, Harvard Business School, who was president of PepsiCo for fifteen years and before that a managing director of McKinsey & Company, says (1988: 99):

What distinguishes outstanding competitors from the rest? Two basic principles. First, they understand that consistent innovation is the key to a company's survival. Being innovative some of the time in one or two areas, just won't work. Second, they know that the most powerful changes they can make are those that create value for their customers and potential customers. The result? Competitive companies constantly look for ways to change every aspect of their business. Then, when they've found them, they make sure that they translate those changes into advantages customers will appreciate and act on.

Peter Drucker, a famous scholar of the American business scene, points out that opportunities to innovate can arise *within* the company as well as outside the company. The areas within the company include unexpected occurrences, incongruities, process needs, and industry and market changes. Drucker illustrates an unexpected occurrence. A German scientist synthesized novocaine, the first nonaddictive narcotic. He had intended it for use

Table 5.1
CEO and PR Specialists' Rankings of Corporate Reputation Attributes*

	PR Average Rank	CEO's Average Rank
1. Quality of Products and Services	1.5	1.75
2. Quality of Management	2.5	4.1
3. Financial Soundness	3.7	5.2
4. Ability to Attract and Keep Talented People	3.8	5.2
5. Innovativeness	4.8	2.8
6. Long-Term Investment Value	5.4	3.2
7. Community and Environment Responsibility	6.4	7.6
8. Use of Corporate Assets	7.5	5.2

*These are the eight attributes covered in the <u>Fortune</u> reputation surveys.

in surgical procedures such as amputation. Surgeons preferred total anesthesia for this procedure, but novocaine found a great market among dentists.

An example of incongruities between expectations and results can make it imperative to innovate. In the ocean freighter industry, ships were made faster and more economical in terms of gas consumption; however, these freighters were not making a profit. Eventually, the industry realized that their highest expense came from the hours and days the ships were idle in port. As a result of this realization, the roll on and roll off ship and the container ship were invented.

The third opportunity pointed out by Drucker is process needs. In the early 1900s AT&T projected that because of the great increase in the U.S. population and in telephone use, by 1920 every woman in the United States would have to be employed as a telephone operator to work the switchboards. So, the company was forced to invent an automatic switching process.

The final type of opportunity within a company or industry mentioned by Drucker is industry and market changes. When these changes arise, they provide an opportunity for innovators to come into the market while older firms tend to continue to do business as usual.

One external factor that leads to innovation is demographic change. Drucker cites the Japanese interest in robotics as an example. They knew that the baby bust and the increasing level of education would lead to a sharp decrease in blue-collar workers for the 1990s and beyond.

Another external factor is perception. For example, even though Americans have experienced increases in longevity, they are more and more interested in health improvements. Thus the market for exercise equipment and health food has expanded.

Finally, new knowledge can lead to innovation if entrepreneurs can see how it can be adapted. The development of the personal computer has led to many business coups. American Hospital Supply furnished personal computers free of charge to its customers so that they could send orders when their hospital supply stocks were running out. The devices were so easy to use and became so popular that competitors had great difficulty selling products to hospitals with the American Hospital Supply equipment.

The mechanisms to keep on innovating often show that companies that are leaders in industry are working to "obsolete" their own best products. They see that if they do not come up with the new products their competitors will. Paul Cook (Taylor 1990: 87–106) says that pressure is needed to keep people making the company innovative. He advises "management by calling about." The CEO should contact people and see how their experiments went and what products they are working with. He also advises that people within the company speak to each other and share ideas. Constant innovation means the testing time for products could narrow.

Cook was asked the following question: "So, companies are not just selling innovation, they're selling confidence that they will stand behind the innovation?" He responded as follows:

Absolutely. Many customers have stuck their necks out to buy products from us that they have never seen before. That means we get into trouble from time to time. But, I can't remember one case where this organization didn't rally day and night as long as it took to solve the problem. In fact, when you have those experiences, customers always wind up more friendly, more favorably disposed towards the next innovation. That's not the way we intend to do business, but it's part of the territory."

Since there will be constant change, information about change will have to be communicated to the consumer. Certainly, helping in the handling of communication about innovation and new product problems would be an excellent area for public relations specialists and public relations professionals to "spread their wings" in the next few decades.

Long-term investment value was chosen as the third most important corporate reputation attribute by the CEOs, while the PR personnel ranked this attribute sixth. The PR people did not ignore financial aspects as they ranked financial soundness third. What this may point to is the fact that the CEO really focuses on the market value of the company and on the long-term viability of the firm. In Chapter 6, we discuss some of the benefits of keeping the CEO for a long-term period. This long-term view is very important to keeping companies strong.

CEOs ranked quality of management fourth while PR personnel ranked it second in our study. It seems that the CEOs interviewed by us are underrating the importance of their own work. Overall, when *Fortune* asked its own raters, who participated in the *Fortune* survey, quality of management was rated first and quality of product second. We must again emphasize that these are average (mean) scores. There was considerably more divergence in the rankings chosen by the different CEOs versus those of the public relations people.

The next rankings by the CEOs (table 5.1) were a tie for financial soundness, ability to attract and keep talented people, and use of corporate assets. Except for the wise use of corporate assets, the PR specialists had ranked these variables much higher.

Community and environmental responsibility were ranked last by CEOs and next to last by PR personnel.

Although environment and social responsibility rank low on ratings for factors that affect reputation, if trouble arises a very swift "turnaround" in reputation ratings can take place. This type of emergency may indicate the need for special priorities for CEOs and PR professionals. A good example is the problem faced by Union Carbide in 1984.

In December 1984, an explosion at a Union Carbide plant in Bhopal, India, killed more than 2,500 people. Immediately afterward, Union Carbide received as many as 5,000 calls per day from the press. As reported in the *Economist* on March 18, 1989, it seems that although the company had cultivated its relationship with environmental groups, it had largely ignored journalists. After Bhopal, the company was lambasted by the media. Union Carbide appointed a senior public relations manager who talked to the chair every day. His job was to improve media relations and to help employees feel proud to work for the company. Another task was to avoid a takeover by trying to raise stock prices. Communications—broadly defined—now takes up 75 percent of the chair's time.

Today, many European companies are reshaping their boards so that the chief executive is responsible for day-to-day business, leaving the chair to act as ambassador for the company. According to Sir John Harvey-Jones, former chief executive at ICI, a British chemicals giant, the main activities with which a company chair should be concerned are strategic planning and public relations (1989: 67–68). Other firms that cannot spare so much time of the CEO for communications have appointed an experienced public relations manager as manager of corporate communications. This person sits between the finance director and the CEO and talks with them every day. In addition, this individual should sit in on the company's executive committees to see how decisions are made and to advise on their impact.

Another area of social responsibility besides environmental issues is the problem of workers' family commitments. Robert

Haas, CEO of Levi Strauss & Co., says (Howard 1990: 138), "if employees aren't worrying about things outside the workplace, if they feel supported—not just financially but 'psychologically'—then they are going to be more responsive to the needs of customers and of the business. That support needs to come in a whole set of managerial areas: supervisory practices, peer relations, training, work organization, access to information and the like." Levi Strauss allows a wide group of workers to make up policies to handle these problems.

In the area of corporate responsibility, many corporations contribute to charities on a nationwide or community basis. What is the most effective way to contribute? Richard Haayen, former CEO of Allstate, feels that the best contributions are to support worker activities in the community. This makes for an excellent image for the company and allows the employees to be involved. For example, during a flood the Allstate workers went to the scene of the flood and provided food and aid to the flood victims. The company provided funds for this aid and furnished the workers with Allstate caps. This fostered a spirit of unity among the workers and also provided publicity for Allstate. The company won many awards and enhanced their reputation through this type of activity. We have seen examples of this type of work in the company groups who work for telephone fund drives such as the Muscular Dystrophy Association and the Public Broadcasting System.

CEO SUGGESTIONS FOR BUILDING CORPORATE REPUTATION FOR EACH OF THE EIGHT ATTRIBUTES

In our survey CEOs were asked to rank the eight aspects of corporate reputation used by the *Fortune* reputation studies and discuss what they did about them. In addition, a number of the top executives were interviewed by *Fortune* in 1986 with regard to what they do to enhance corporate reputation in each of the eight areas. In table 5.1 above, we saw how our executives rate each of the *Fortune* categories; table 5.2 lists some of the ways the

Table 5.2

CEOs' Suggestions of Actions to Build Corporate Reputations in the Areas of the Eight Attributes Used in the *Fortune* Studies

Key Attributes	Actions to Enhance
1. Financial Soundness (Coca-Cola)*	1. Maximize shareholder return
	2. Measure managers in terms of value-added (after tax operating profits means cost of capital to acquire earnings).
2. Value as Long-Term Investment (Philip Morris)	1. Cut costs so profits rise.
	2. Acquire strong firms.
3. Use of Corporate Assets (Berkshire Hathaway)	1. Buy shares in companies whose value is higher than market price.
4. Innovativeness (3M)	1. Establish global lines to investors in all countries.
	2. Establish two-tier promotion systems (inventors who don't manage may get pay and perks of a VP).
	3. Urge technical people to swap information throughout the firm.
	4. Insist that 25% sales come from products developed in past 5 years.
5. Ability to Attract and Keep Talented Workers (Exxon, Procter and Gamble, Merck)	1. Have CEO interview applicants on college campuses.
	2. Expect older star employees to recruit new stars.
	3. Encourage worker's outside activities.
	4. Provide for quick promotions.
	5. Promote from within.
	6. Executive development.
6. Quality of Products or Services (Rubbermaid)	1. Encourage good manufacturing.
	2. Expect good service.
	3. Encourage attractive product design.
	4. Check product quality constantly.
7. Quality of Management (Wal-Mart)	1. Treat workers like entrepreneurs.
	2. Get ideas from workers.
	3. Communicate well.
	4. Provide managers with detailed financial statements, cost and profit margins.
8. Community and Environmental Responsibility (Johnson & Johnson, Procter & Gamble)	1. Keep ethics high.
	2. Stress honesty, integrity.
	3. Put people before profits.
	4. Sponsor employee benefits. (housing, daycare)
	5. Withdraw products that might have defects.

*The names of the companies in parentheses indicate that these are suggestions of CEOs of these companies as reported in "Two CEOs Talk About Corporate Reputations," *Fortune* January 6, 1986 p. 20 and "Leaders of the Most Admired," *Fortune* January 29, 1990, pp. 40-54.

executives interviewed by *Fortune* enhance their reputations.

WHAT CAN A GOOD REPUTATION DO FOR A COMPANY?

There are several areas where a good reputation can help the company. These are categorized in table 5.3. In the labor market one may be able to hire better workers for lower salaries (Tsui 1984; Schwoerer and Rosen 1989). Financing may be easier for the company with a good image. Product sales may be facilitated and may require less advertising. Community relationships may be easier and zoning and "tax breaks" may be more accessible for the "good company." We asked the CEOs to rank a number of possible benefits in these four areas. Table 5.3 shows the results of their ratings and compares them to the ratings of the PR practitioners and consultants.

In the view of our respondents, of the twenty choices regarding benefits of a good reputation, only one was of the "utmost importance": better quality of workers (1.5). Our PR practitioners and professionals agreed on this issue.

At the opposite end of the importance spectrum, the benefits regarded as least important were less expensive benefit plans possible (4.3) and less restriction on selling bonds (4.3).

The results in table 5.3 are useful from many points of view. It is interesting, of course, to see the CEO ratings on all twenty choices of positive effects of good reputation. But, in addition, the categorizing scheme may be helpful to companies in targeting goals for specific advertising and public relations plans. Firms can prioritize their goals by looking at the list of potential benefits. Then they can develop plans designed to provide the select benefits they have targeted.

When the rankings of the CEOs and PR people are compared, they follow similar patterns. For example in the labor area, better quality of workers is ranked highest by both groups followed by increased employee loyalty and larger selection of potential employees.

Table 5.3
Comparison of PR Specialists' and CEO Rating of What a Good Corporate Image Can Do for a Company

	PR Average Ratings	CEOs Average Ratings
Labor		
Larger selection of potential employees	2.1	2.0
Better quality of workers	1.2	1.5
Increased employee loyalty	2.0	2.0
Lower wage rates possible	4.4	3.8
Less expensive benefit plans possible	4.1	4.3
Finance		
Ability to float more loans	2.2	4.0
Lower interest rate on loans	3.1	3.8
Less restriction on selling bonds	4.1	4.3
Ability to issue stock at higher prices	3.0	4.0
Ability to sell more stock	1.9	3.5
Product/Service Sales		
Ability to sell high quantities	2.7	2.3
Ability to charge higher prices	2.2	3.7
Ability to devote less $ to advertising	4.1	3.7
Ability to expand product line	2.7	3.3
Ability to sell through more dealers	2.5	2.0
Community		
Ability to locate in better communities	4.2	3.3
Increased possibility for business extensions	2.4	3.8
Ability to deal with local governments	2.9	2.5
Ability to obtain media coverage	3.0	2.5
Ability to establish consumer trust	1.4	2.0

The highest rating is 1 (utmost importance) and the lowest rating is 5 (not important).

In the finance area, according to both the PR personnel and the CEOs, the highest rating was accorded to ability to sell more stock and the lowest was accorded to less restriction on selling bonds. In the product/service sales area, ability to charge higher prices is rated first by the PR personnel (2.2), while the CEOs rank it last (3.7). The CEOs pick ability to sell through more dealers as more important. There is much divergence on product/service sales.

Finally, in the community area, *both* CEOs and PR people agreed that ability to establish consumer trust is the most important community aspect of what a good rating can do for a company.

Thus, as we compare PR rankings and CEO rankings they seem to rate the outcomes similarly—but there are two exceptions.

First, the PR people give all the outcomes of what good reputation can do for the company higher ratings than the CEOs do. (Note in table 5.3 that each individual interviewee was asked to rate the importance of the outcomes of good reputation on a scale of 1 to 5, with 1 being very important and 5 being least important.) It seems from our study that PR professionals and practitioners are more impressed with the value of a good reputation than are CEOs. It would "make sense" that the PR people would have a higher opinion of the importance of their work.

This finding seems to be at odds with a recent study of opinions about how public relations contribute to profits. According to a recent article in the *Wall Street Journal*, executive respondents gave PR a 235 percent return-on-investment rating. More modest PR chiefs gave themselves a 205 percent ROI rating, in the six-year, $400,000 study. (This statistic was also quoted by Laressa Grunig in a speech to the International Association of Business Communicators (IABC), Dallas, Texas, February 13, 1991.)

POSSIBLE LESSONS FROM THE IN-DEPTH STUDY

Once again, as we noted earlier in this chapter, the CEO opinions tended to be more divergent than the opinions of PR practitioners and PR professionals. In some cases, they emphasized different points.

Some reflections on these issues might indicate possible communication problems between CEOs and PR professionals. These might include the following possibilities:

1. It is important to get the "right chemistry" between CEOs and PR professionals.
2. It must be somewhat difficult for the two groups to "get along," given their different philosophies. Could this explain why companies often switch from one public relations firm to another?
3. Do CEOs expect too much from the PR people and their PR plans? CEOs may have exalted views of their firms and may not understand

the time commitment necessary to carry out the plans and to receive positive returns.

4. Perhaps the PR group lacks vision to a certain extent. Maybe they should be more innovative, considering more options, mechanisms, and avenues of communication.

5. What could the groups learn by talking to each other? Maybe the CEOs would become more focused, the PR groups more open to a wide variety of techniques.

6. Could it be that the aims of CEOs are long-term in nature and those of the PRs shorter-term? We have some intimation of this in table 5.1, where the CEOs rank long-term investment value much higher than PR professionals do.

Before the companies and their PR professionals communicate to the public, it seems evident that they should communicate with each other. The solutions discussed previously in this chapter, where the chair of the board devotes a large percent of time to public relations or where the PR chief has offices next door to the CEO and talks with the CEO daily would help handle this problem.

There is much to be learned from the comments our survey elicited from both the public relations professionals and the CEOs. Putting their words into action—the real challenge—is the topic we explore in the remaining chapters of this book.

CHAPTER 6

Building a Good Reputation as a Help in Attracting Quality Workers

In the CEO and PR specialist surveys both groups were asked to rank the *Fortune* corporate reputation attributes. For the PR people the ability to attract and keep talented people was in fourth place. For the CEOs this attribute tied with financial soundness and wise use of corporate assets for fifth place. Thus ability to attract and keep workers is of middling importance to good corporate reputation. Yet it is probably a key factor in running a successful business. What can a good corporate reputation actually do for a firm in the labor field?

According to the Tavistock Institute (Mason 1980) there are eight characteristics that determine the psychological attractiveness of a job. These are as follows:

1. A job should be somewhat demanding and bring out the complexity of the individual.
2. A job should have some degree of optimum variety so that one does not do the same things over and over.
3. A job should provide a sense of completion.

4. One should have ability to go on learning on the job.
5. A job should provide the autonomy to make decisions and discretion to control the activities upon which one works.
6. A job should provide some kind of social support system from one's coworkers.
7. People should be able to relate what they do and what they produce to their social life.
8. People should believe that their job leads to some sort of desirable future for them.

The CEO recommendations from *Fortune* interviews start with two ideas to attract good workers. These ideas (listed in table 5.2) include having the CEO interview applicants on college campuses and asking older star employees to recruit new stars. The Tavistock attributes listed above do not cover recruiting; they refer only to job attributes. One would assume, however, that older star employees or CEOs who have worked "their way up" in the business would be in a good position to stress many of the job attributes of employment in their company outlined by the Tavistock Institute.

The next three items covered in table 5.2 do fit the Tavistock classifications. The first suggestion is to encourage the workers' outside activities, which would relate to Tavistock point 7. The next two items suggested by CEOs include provision for quick promotions and promotions from within, which would coordinate with Tavistock point number 8. Similarly, CEO suggestion 6, which advocates executive development, would help workers build a desirable future for themselves and would match Tavistock goal 4.

We turn now to suggestions for attracting and retaining good workers that have been advocated in the recent financial, news, and popular media. We have seen in the first two qualities advocated in the Tavistock study that good jobs bring out the complexity of the individual and provide an optimum amount of variety. To meet this need, we suggest that good employers prize originality in every form. Not only does this increase ability to attract employees, but creative and different approaches attract the attention of investors, customers, the financial press, and the media in general. This enables the firm to get free publicity. Firms that are not creative pay for their publicity. Looking at ways in which firms have earned free publicity in the past may be helpful to start deliberations about future strategies. Yet such techniques are of limited usefulness only, since the future is never exactly like the past and also because the goal of being creative relates to finding new solutions, rather than continuing to use the tried and true ones. Nevertheless, picking up a current business periodical and scanning it for mention of creative firms may be a good starting point for thought and action.

ENCOURAGING CREATIVITY IN MANY AREAS

Creative Annual Reports

Some firms include a sample of their product, provide video reports, or offer a premium to investors (who reach a certain point in reading the report and read the buried message telling them that they qualify for a premium), or use some other technique to make their reports stand out in the vast amount of financial report material produced annually by corporations. It is overwhelming to think of the financial and human resources spent on producing annual report material (most with glossy covers and fancy photography)—much of which is probably unread and underappreciated.

There must be a better way of getting financial data communicated and the corporate "message" across to the market. This is a challenge that awaits a forward-looking company that is not afraid to take the initiative and provide a different, inexpensive way of communicating vital facts to the outside world. We live in a world in which the range of communication mechanisms has greatly expanded and continues to do so; and yet most firms have continued to issue the staid, boring, expensive annual report that most recipients immediately toss into the garbage heap! How about a faxed one-page report with an application form for additional information?

Debbie Galant (1990: 124–126) provides some interesting examples of innovative approaches to communicating with the financial community and investors:

- Ben & Jerry's Homemade, the Ice Cream Company, included in its 1988 annual report a social audit, verified by an "independent social auditor." Among other things the report notes Ben & Jerry's socially responsible attitudes toward industrial waste (waste ice cream is sometimes fed to local pigs) and recycling (yellow paper and gummed message pads are banned because they cannot be recycled).

- Quaker Oats Co.'s first quarter 1990 report contains a special sixteen-page insert, titled "Nutrition and Wellness," giving the company's response to the recent medical backlash about the link between oat bran and cholesterol. The report includes a bibliography of cholesterol research, a special feature on how to read a food label, a history of the Food and Drug Administration's position on product health claims, and other information about cholesterol in Q&A format.

- To launch its new software package, "Word for Windows," Microsoft Corporation sent to computer-publication editors and industry watchers a six-part (in installments!) audiocassette soap opera, "As the Word Turns."

- Along with its second-quarter 1989 report, California Energy Co. sent investors an empty matchbook with this message: "Geothermal energy . . . is matchless."

- Xtra Corporation, a Boston truck-leasing company, ran a television commercial (on the Financial News Network) as part of a proxy contest. The commercial attracted quite a bit of attention. "Good Morning, America" and *USA Today* ran stories about it.

Community Service

Community service can help convince the public that the firm is a good corporate citizen and worthy of their business and support.

The Southland Corporation (7 Eleven) with its support of the Muscular Dystrophy Association shows how employees can contribute to a national program.

Motivating and Rewarding Employees

Consumers often have a positive response to companies that treat their employees well for two reasons: First, unhappy in the treatment they receive on their own jobs, they may identify with employees and approve of, and want to buy from, companies that treat their employees in a better than average fashion. Second, they may think (and most likely, correctly) that satisfied employees provide better products and services and thus they may be eager to buy from such a company. Ideas that fall in these categories could be day care centers, special vacations, monetary awards, flexible hours, and educational benefits.

New Products

Remember that the best way to make money and stay ahead of the crowd is to be different—and right! Proof of this was recently provided by Procter & Gamble, whose scientists invented a combination shampoo-conditioner, now marketed as "Pert Plus." In the beginning, (Swasy 1990: B1), management was unimpressed, but now the brand is the leading shampoo, "with about 12% of the fragmented $1.4 billion U.S. market, where more than 1,100 products compete." Competitors are now copying it.

This clearly seems to be a case of a company's deserving a good reputation, because apparently it created a product that consumers really needed and wanted. Too often, it is the reverse. The product is created and then the public needs to be convinced of its efficacy. According to Alecia Swasy, B1, "The success of a Pert Plus demonstrates one of the oldest marketing truisms: Consumers flock to true innovations, regardless of slick advertising or fancy packages. P&G nearly overlooked its Seattle test market of Pert Plus, investing little for advertising and promotions. But consumers swarmed to the product, doubling sales within six months."

What is interesting also is that P&G has not needed a glitzy advertising campaign tailored for each market. One campaign by ad agency Leo Burnett in Chicago serves thirty-one markets. The ad is a simple one—a testimonial hyping the "wash and go" convenience of Pert Plus. It is interesting to reflect on the fact that some appeals—such as the one to save consumer time—span all cultures.

Brainstorming

It could be helpful to have different kinds of brainstorming sessions: one in which new ideas are generated and built upon, with no criticizing and no practicality permitted; and another with a much more practical bent, where total emphasis is on the creation of useful, unique ideas, with no "blue skying" allowed.

There are lots of different sources that are appropriate for generating a successful brainstorming session. A series of quotations from any source (books, magazines, newspapers, etc.) might be helpful in generating ideas relevant to the firm's business. The page of quotations at the back of *Forbes* magazine could be useful. It might be interesting to reflect on a quote such as that on a flyer written by L. L. Bean in 1912: "I do not consider the sale a success until the goods are worn out and the customer still satisfied." Clay Carr (1990) considers this to be the single best description of total quality ever written.

Another area ripe for brainstorming purposes is the academic literature. Encourage people to read it. Perhaps guest researchers from nearby colleges could be invited to discuss the latest research. Ideas for the future rest there. They need to be uncovered and put to use. A company can support research by academics or joint research with academics and some of its own people. Such research can help a company find ways to improve business; it might earn the company good publicity as well. The important thing is to devise ways of staying at the forefront of knowledge in your own field.

At times, brainstorming may lead to some good ideas and other times it may not. But at the very least, it should help to energize the staff, keep them thinking along positive lines, and constantly remind them that they are an important part of a group effort. This brainstorming would help to carry out points 1–5 of the Tavistock good job characteristics.

EMPOWERING EMPLOYEES TO PROVIDE GOOD SERVICE

The fifth point advocated by Tavistock is that "a job should provide the autonomy to make decisions and discretion to control the activities upon which one works." Recently this idea has been developed in novel ways by companies eager to improve the quality of their service. The new policy *is to empower employees at all levels to provide quality service.* In order to do this it may be necessary to cut down on the degree of specialization in the firm.

Specialization of labor has numerous benefits; but one important cost is that employees can feel somewhat removed from overall service goals of the company. Dedicated to their own individual tasks, employees may not see how their work is part of a larger whole. This kind of a dissected whole can create many holes—holes into which dissatisfied customers fall.

In a recent article in the *Wall Street Journal* Ray Schultz, president and chief executive officer of Hampton Inn Hotels, offers one solution to this dilemma. In October, 1989, Hampton Inn instituted a guarantee, stated as follows: "if our guests have a problem or complaint at any time during their stay, and are not satisfied when they leave, we'll give them one night's stay for free." What is especially unique about this guarantee is that it can be fulfilled by any regular employee who deals with customers. According to Schultz, it is not just managers or front desk personnel who are empowered to take whatever action is necessary to keep customers satisfied. He cites the example of a housekeeper who notices that a guest is getting frustrated because his key won't work in the door: "Instead of simply referring the problem to the front desk or calling the maintenance department, the housekeeper will take responsibility for getting a new key, changing the lock or arranging for a different room. If the guest still isn't happy, the housekeeper may offer to refund the cost of the room for the night—without contacting the manager" (Schultz 1991: A16). This policy makes sense, because all of us have suffered frustration at the hands of employees who are polite and pleasant but lack the power to help us with our service problems. Given a choice, in many cases we would probably prefer power to politeness!

Apparently the Hampton Inn policy is working. Schultz reports that, of the guests who invoke the guarantee (getting reimbursed for a night's stay; it is not a voucher for later use) before leaving the hotel, 86 percent say they will return and 45 percent of them already have. The staff seems more motivated too. According to Schultz, "Empowerment is keeping us young—by helping to ward off the sagging standards and slumping morale that can accompany age." This type of empowerment also satisfies quality 3 in Tavistock list.

MOTIVATING WORKERS

Along with empowerment employers should continually look for ways to motivate workers. The eighth quality provided by Tavistock is that "people should believe that their job leads to some sort of desirable future for them." This may involve promises of rewards for the present as well as a secure and well-rewarded future.

Nothing can be more productive and more conducive to a good reputation than a motivated workforce. We all know how hard we can work when we are motivated; all of us, at one time or another, have experienced that very satisfying feeling of knowing we are working to our very top capacity on a meaningful project. That kind of feeling produces a natural "high" in the body and in the intellect that is similar to the high experienced by runners and/or those engaged in aerobic exercise. It has been demonstrated medically that, in certain situations, a burst of adrenaline in the bloodstream can energize people enough to surmount major physical obstacles. In the same vein, companies may be able to create working environments that will energize their workers to accomplish amazing feats—of either the physical or mental variety. Learning to "press the right button" to motivate employees could put a company far ahead of its competitors.

Although reams of text have been written on motivation by psychologists and organizational specialists, it is a subject that still is totally mysterious. A recent article in the *Wall Street Journal* (Smith 1989: A8) illustrates this point. The author shows a juggler and ponders on what it is that motivates him to learn, and excel at, this unusual skill, particularly since it provides little financial reward. The answer is elusive—just as elusive as it is to discover what motivates anyone to do any job. Nevertheless, the company that could excel in motivating would probably excel in creating profits as well.

A recent letter to the editor in the *Wall Street Journal* brings home the crucial importance of motivation in providing quality goods and services:

While organizational experts cry their hearts out emphasizing that the most important asset of a company is its human resources (i.e., its employees), the decimation and demoralization of the American work force during the 1980s by a spectrum of companies have made their (surviving) employees very bitter. . . . Quality of product or service is the result of actions of *motivated* employees. (Subramanian 1990: A11)

A firm might offer a system of immediate rewards for jobs well done, money saved. Other rewards might include stock owner-ship, which helps employees to feel that they really have a vested interest in *their* firm.

Another way to encourage employee loyalty is to give workers the feeling that they have a long-term future with the firm. We saw in the Schwoerer–Rosen study (1989) in chapter 3 that companies that gave assurance that they would fire people only "for cause" were much better able to recruit new workers than those with an "employment-at-will" policy. To maintain this sort of long-term confidence the company should always have a clear long-term view and should have personnel policies that emphasize longevity.

KEEPING THE LONG TERM IN VIEW

Short-term demands never let up; at times it may be tempting to concentrate on them, to the neglect of the long term. Firms do this, as well as individuals. Organizational experts tell us that innovative activity (which is most often long-term in nature and provides no built-in deadlines) can be ruled out by routine activities (which most often are accompanied by short-term deadlines and day-to-day progress). Firms can go out of business if this happens. Perhaps a certain time of the day, the week, the month, and/or the year needs to be devoted to a discussion and consideration of long-term goals (creating and maintaining a good reputation, for example), so that these goals do not get pushed to the background under the pressure of short-term work.

A firm must, of course, be concerned with its short-term plans and reputation, but it must not let these short-term plans demand 100 percent of its attention, or it is doomed for the long term. A good analogy of this can be seen in the sports scene. For example, in college football, rankings change on a weekly basis, with the very latest performance the major input for the most recent rankings. Perceptions change on a weekly basis; what counts, in the long run, is who has the best record at the end of the season. In the same vein, corporations need to be concerned, but not overly so, with short-term variations in their perceived success and reputation rankings. Like baseball teams, companies experience streaks, both winning and losing ones. The challenge is to survive the streaks without abandoning long-term goals. This is a delicate balancing act; because if they do not weather the bad streaks well enough, they will not be around to enjoy the long term!

One wonders if long-term management is possible in the current environment. The trend seems to be in the opposite direction. According to studies by executive recruiters Heidrick & Struggles Inc. in Chicago (Bennett 1990), chief executives' average tenure, which was 7.6 years in 1977, was only 6.4 years in 1987. Even 7.6 years seems like a short amount of time; and the fact that it has fallen lower over the past ten years seems ominous. It is difficult to see how a "long-term" leadership plan could be developed and implemented in a period shorter than eight years. And this is in spite of the fact that there is some evidence that long-term executives may be more effective leaders. The research of Graef Crystal, a professor at the Haas School of Business at the University of California at Berkeley, shows that companies with veterans of twenty or more years at the helm have given investors an average annual return of 18.3 percent since 1970; this compares with a 14.1 percent for all large companies. According to Crystal, "CEOs, like wine, do improve with age" (Alpert 1990: 10). In any event, no matter how long (or short) the tenure of the CEO, it is important that some sort of long-term "vision" be retained at the firm.

DEVELOPING PERSONNEL POLICIES THAT STRESS LONGEVITY

Turnover is a problem for many businesses, but not many firms are willing to make the kind of long-term commitment that would have a lasting effect on this issue. Apparently Merrill Lynch & Co. is an exception, as reported recently in the *Wall Street Journal* *(Siconolfi 1990: C1):*

The nation's largest securities firm will give brokers more incentive to stay with Merrill Lynch over the long haul: Those who remain for 10 years will become eligible for the first time to receive bonuses of $100,000 or more. The firm will also offer new brokers a guaranteed salary for their first two years, to reduce the chances they will sell products just to drum up business.

At the same time, Merrill Lynch is revamping its broker training program. Starting next year, the firm will expand by two years the length of its initial training program for brokers. The training period now is about 20 weeks.

It is interesting that, as Siconolfi reports, Merrill Lynch's training program comes at a time when other Wall Street firms have cut back on hiring fledgling brokers. This is a good example of a firm's willingness to invest in a very valuable asset—its people. This is the kind of investment that probably will be costly as far as immediate effects on the income statement are concerned; but it will probably increase the reputation of Merrill Lynch in the eyes of the public, who are eager to deal with a better educated broker motivated to stay with the firm for the long haul. In the long term, the success of the program should spell success in terms of profit.

Since reputation as a good employer can help a company get a fine staff, it should try to develop personnel policies that show it to be a good employer. We have shown that empowering workers to handle jobs thoroughly, encouraging workers to provide new ideas, and using these ideas where they are effective can increase worker satisfaction. There are employee benefits such as sabbaticals and flexible scheduling that may also build a company's reputation as a good employer.

Great Western, in recruiting, uses its *Fortune* reputation standing. In a recent Great Western ad (*Wall Street Journal*, July 18, 1990, p. B6) it is stated that REPUTATION IS EVERYTHING. The ad announces to potential employees:

FORTUNE WAS RIGHT. According to FORTUNE's 1990 corporate reputations survey, Great Western is ranked as, "the number one corporation among all banks, thrifts and diversified financial institutions."

Although we often develop reputation to cater to specific parties—employees, suppliers, customers, investors—in reality there is a carryover or halo effect. Reputation as a good employer may "rub off" and help to create a good reputation as judged by consumers and/or the stock market. And, rightly so, because an advantage in the labor market will have spillover effects, ultimately creating better and/or cheaper products and hence higher returns for investors.

CHAPTER 7

Building a Reputation for Quality of Products and Services

As previously mentioned, *Fortune* (Sprout 1991) notes that when respondents in the corporate reputation survey pick which attribute is most important in the determination of corporate reputation each year, more than 80 percent of them pick quality of management as paramount. Quality of a company's products or services has consistently ranked as the second most significant factor; however, in the most recent survey, Alison L. Sprout notes that product/service quality is now moving closer to quality of management as the most important element in corporate reputation. Our survey of both CEOs and PR personnel placed the quality of products and services as the number one corporate reputation attribute. The product quality was far and away the most important issue, ranking at least one point higher than any other item. Product and service quality is probably going to be the most important issue of the 1990s. Stanley C. Gault, CEO and chair of the board of Rubbermaid, the company considered to have the highest reputation for quality of products or services in 1990, stresses four actions to enhance quality of products:

1. Encourage good manufacturing
2. Expect good service
3. Encourage attractive product design
4. Check product quality constantly

These exhortations represent only the "tip of the iceberg." Quality has been an important topic in government and industry circles since the early 1980s. In order to encourage greater productivity and competitiveness, President Reagan signed legislation calling for a national study conference on productivity in October 1982. About this time Alvin O. Gunneson, corporate vice president of quality for Revlon, and the American Society for Quality Control had formed in February 1982, the National Advisory Council for Quality (NACQ) (DeCarlo and Sterett 1990). The council was a broad-based group of private and public sector executives committed to quality. The NACQ aimed to be a center for training, publications, conferences, and research in quality disciplines.

There were similar efforts by the American Productivity and Quality Center (APQC), formerly the American Productivity Center, founded by C. Grayson Jackson, former member of the National Price Control Board and former dean of the business school of Southern Methodist University. The APQC was a nonprofit organization committed to improving productivity, quality, and competitiveness. This organization raised $1 million to pay for the conference, which received and coordinated ideas by computer networking sessions from 175 corporate executives, business leaders, and academicians. One of the major outcomes of this conference was the suggestion for a national quality award similar to the Deming Prize in Japan. The White House Conference on Productivity, in 1984, pointed to the fact that U. S. growth in productivity had faltered and suggested that a national medal for productivity achievement be awarded annually by the president, to recognize high levels of productivity achievement by organizations. Grayson proposed that although the medal was to be awarded by the president, the winners should be selected by the private sector to avoid political influence. Work on the award was begun in 1985 and by the fall of 1986 draft criteria for the award had been developed by the National Organization for the United States Quality Award, an entirely private sector group of academicians and corporate quality business leaders. Meanwhile, work was being done to establish national legislation for the award. Congressman Don Fuqua (D-Fla.), Congressman Doug Walgren (D-Pa.), and Senator Bob Graham (D-Fla.) were among the supporters of the bill. As Neil J. DeCarlo and W. Kent Sterrett say (1990: 22): "On June 8 (1987), the measure passed the House and was sent to the Senate Committee on Commerce, Science and Transportation. Before the Senate could act, a tragic accident occurred: Commerce Secretary Malcolm Baldrige was killed in a rodeo accident. Three days after Baldrige's death the Senate renamed the legislation in his honor. The bill was sent to the Senate floor and passed. The House unanimously agreed to the amendment and on August 20, 1987, President Reagan signed the Malcolm Baldrige National Quality Improvement Act of 1987 into law."

The three categories of business that are currently covered by the award are manufacturing, service, and small business. Over 180,000 Baldrige applications were requested last year (Fuchsberg 1991). Many companies might not have been interested in applying for the award but wanted to use the criteria to review and reorganize their operations. Companies that have won have used this fact in their advertising to boost sales. In the spring of 1991, for example, Cadillac advertised their prize to boost corporate reputation and sales.

Now the Commerce Department, which administers the Baldrige Award, has been considering taking entries from universities, hospitals, and other nonprofit organizations (Fuchsberg 1991). The schools and hospitals insist that they are working with people and they are service businesses. Currently, the advisory panel that oversees the award is considering seeking congressional approval to expand the award.

Later in this chapter we shall examine the Baldrige award criteria and discuss their relationship to corporate reputation and what actions a firm might take to improve the quality of their services and products.

In our survey we asked both PR specialists and CEOs to rate the benefits of good corporate image in the product and sales fields. CEOs felt that good corporate image and quality would enable a company to sell through more dealers and to sell higher quantities. It could also help a company expand its product line. They were not as likely to feel that it would allow a company to charge higher prices or to devote less money to advertising. The PR specialists felt that the most important value of good image and hence good quality was that it would allow a company to charge higher prices. In addition, it would allow a company to sell through more dealers. In third place was ability to expand product line and ability to sell high quantities (table 5.3).

EMPHASIZING QUALITY SERVICE AND TELLING THE PUBLIC ABOUT IT

CEOs emphasize the importance of product and service quality. Consumerism is crucial. Time is also valued by customers more than ever before. This means that complete, timely, reliable service is an ever-more prized commodity. According to Amanda Bennett (1990: B1, B4), "During the 1980s, the corporate drive for perfection focused on improving the product. Now pursuit of a competitive edge has shifted to honing the caliber of customer care." In this same article, Bennett discusses the results of a recent *Wall Street Journal*/NBC News survey, in which 1,507 consumers were polled on their view of the quality of service provided by U.S. business. The report card, summarized in table 7.1, is not impressive. Although the level of service was rated as excellent or pretty good by 55 percent of the respondents, 44 percent gave a rating of only fair or poor. Unfortunately, the outlook for the future does not seem good. In general the perception is not one of continuing improvement in service. The

Table 7.1
How Business Measures Up

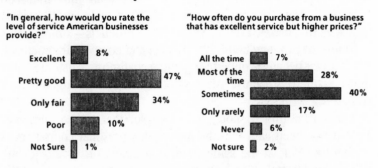

"In general, how would you rate the level of service American businesses provide?"

Excellent	8%
Pretty good	47%
Only fair	34%
Poor	10%
Not Sure	1%

"How often do you purchase from a business that has excellent service but higher prices?"

All the time	7%
Most of the time	28%
Sometimes	40%
Only rarely	17%
Never	6%
Not sure	2%

"How would you rate the overall level of service these industries provide customers?"

	GETTING BETTER	GETTING WORSE	STAYING ABOUT THE SAME	NOT SURE
Supermarkets	31%	18%	50%	1%
Automobiles	24	37	31	8
Restaurants	22	19	56	3
Department stores	20	29	48	3
Hotels	20	16	45	19
Banks	17	29	50	4
Airlines	11	36	40	13
Insurance	10	49	34	7
Gas Stations	6	59	32	3

Source: Amanda Bennett, <u>Wall Street Journal</u>, November 12, 1990, p. B1

total of percentages in the "getting worse" category is much higher than the total in the "getting better" column. Interestingly, consumers are not unalterably opposed to paying higher prices for excellent service.

It is hard to see why businesses cannot provide what consumers are willing to buy. Yet Bennett reports that Forum Corp., a Boston consulting firm, has data to indicate that "two of five customers who stop doing business with a company do so over service-related issues, while only 8% leave because of price and another 8% for poor-quality products."

In discussing a 1989 report of a *Wall Street Journal* survey of the aspirations and attitudes of more than four thousand consumers from all walks of life, Alix M. Freedman (1989: B4) indicates that people crave "Anxiety-free products—simple items without lots of fancy bells and whistles and complex instructions. It's not just because souped-up gizmos cost more. Customers just don't want to squander their mental energy figuring out how something works."

It is interesting to note, for example, that in the computer field it has been said that the market for personal computers is drying up. Yet, at the same time, consumers are afraid to buy computers because they will not know how to work them. John Rossi, president of Blue Chip International Inc., which makes IBM compatible computers, has commented (Freedman 1989: B4) "Generally, we talk in what, for most people, amounts to a foreign language. The only problem is the computer industry doesn't know it." It is amazing to think that businesses smart enough to master computer technology are not clever enough to provide consumers with what they really want! Clearly, there is a problem here. The real demand (for simplicity of product, for service, etc.) is not being met. One of the principles of Marketing 101 is to first find out the demand and then fill it, but business does not seem to work this way!

As mentioned previously, reputation is a topic that spans many different fields of endeavor. Nowhere is this more evident than in the area of quality service, because, regardless of corporate directives, such service will not be provided by disgruntled and unhappy employees.

So here we enter the realm of the ability of management to motivate employees on a continuous basis. If good management and good service are inexorably tied, and reputation requires good service, then good management and good reputation are tied as well. To borrow a refrain from the old song, "You can't have one without the other." It may be possible to monitor, to a certain extent, the quality of service provided by employees. But all of the service cannot be monitored, only some of it. Regardless of supervisory techniques and layers of bonuses and incentives, employees are still left with many opportunities to make or break the firm by delivering quality service or by not paying attention to quality service. It is up to management to create an environment in which employees will be motivated to provide good service, in the presence or absence of monitoring. A good example of this is provided by the Walt Disney Company, where employees are sent to Disney College to learn the principles of dealing with the public.

According to Ron Zemke (Bennett 1990: B1), president of Performance Research Associates Inc., a consulting firm in Minneapolis, businesses that find they are not viewed as service-oriented "try to advertise that they are, to convince customers that they are." They work on the perception, rather than the reality. Zemke comments: "The last thing they do is to do the hard work, and go through and see where the systems don't work." Although these efforts may have some transitory results, they probably do not contribute to the long-term reputation of the firm.

A renewed emphasis on quality is being made by numerous firms, and organizational charts have been revised to reflect this emphasis. Whether the improvement is substantive is questionable.

The pursuit of quality has become a big business. As reported recently in the *Wall Street Journal*, American Express's chair and CEO, James D. Robinson, III, had his directors change company bylaws to give him a third title: chief quality officer. American Express is not the only company telling the world that the pursuit of quality is an important goal. Fuchsberg (1990: B1) reports:

Until recent years, few companies, particularly in the service sector, employed people with the word quality in their titles. Those that did often limited them to monitoring assembly lines, massaging defect rates and checking suggestion boxes.

Now, though, quality officers plot strategy, not charts. And their numbers are growing. Of 52 big companies surveyed recently by recruiters Battalia & Associates Inc., New York, nearly half—including Aetna Life & Casualty Co. and National Semiconductor Corp.—had created executive-level quality posts since 1988."

It is interesting that the attempt, on the part of firms, to deal with concerns about quality, on the practical day-to-day level as well as on the organizational chart, gets increasing attention in the financial press, which indicates that these are items of interest to customers and to investors as well. These are times in which financial facts and figures are of limited use to investors without being supplemented by qualitative developments within the firms that "frame" financial results and aid the investor in interpreting these results. After all, the future is never exactly like the past; financial results deal with the past only, and may or may not be replicated.

Quality of service as well as quality of the product is another very important area covered in the Malcolm Baldrige National Quality Award.

The award has established seven examination categories to evaluate the firms that have applied for awards. Table 7.2 outlines these categories and shows the relative weight of each category over the years since the award started (1988–1991). Table 7.3 shows the subcategories for each of the seven categories that are examined for the awards. It also outlines the point scores for each of these subcategories. The weights for each of these categories has varied, but customer satisfaction has always been the most important criterion. It counts 30 percent of the total one thousand points.

DETERMINING CUSTOMER REQUIREMENTS AND EXPECTATIONS

The first important issue is determining customer requirements and expectations. It is worth thirty points or 10 percent of the score for consumer satisfaction. A quality problem could arise

Table 7.2
Percent Weighting of National Quality Award Examination Categories, 1988–1991

Driver	System	Measure of Progress	Goal
1. Leadership	2. Information & Analyses	6. Quality Results	7. Customer Satisfaction
1988 15%	1988 7.5%	1988 10%	1988 30%
1989 12%	1989 6.0%	1989 15%	1989 30%
1990 10%	1990 6.0%	1990 15%	1990 30%
1991 10%	1991 7.0%	1991 18%	1991 30%
	3. Strategic Quality Planning		
	1988 7.5%		
	1989 8.0		
	1990 9.0		
	1991 6.0		
	4. Human Resources Utilization		
	1988 15.0%		
	1989 15.0%		
	1990 15.0%		
	1991 15.0%		
	5. Quality Assistance of Products and Services		
	1988 15.0%		
	1989 14.0%		
	1990 15.0%		
	1991 14.0%		

Source: DeCarlo and Sterrett, pp. 22, 24, 26.
National Institute of Standards and Technology, 1991
Application Guidelines, p. 5.

because the firm does not determine customer requirements and expectations and, indeed, is not aware of who the customer is.

Very often after products are designed the marketers do not aim their information and advertising at the proper customers. Often ads are targeted to the elite upper class. This is a mistake if the product is designed for nation-wide consumption. According to Al Reis, chair of Trout & Reis, a marketing research firm (Freedman 1989: B4), "Advertising too often reflects the life styles of the creators rather than the consumers of the ads. . . . Marketers are missing the main-stream of America by a mile."

Advertising helps to determine reputation, and if ads appeal to only one group, rather than many, reputation is adversely affected.

Table 7.3
1991 Examination Categories and Items, Malcolm Baldrige National Quality Award

1991 Examination Categories/Items	Maximum Points
1.0 Leadership	**100**
1.1 Senior Executive Leadership....................................40	
1.2 Quality Values...15	
1.3 Management for Quality..25	
1.4 Public Responsibility...20	
2.0 Information and Analysis	**70**
2.1 Scope and Management of Quality Data and Information.........20	
2.2 Competitive Comparisons and Benchmarks......................30	
2.3 Analysis of Quality Data and Information....................20	
3.0 Strategic Quality Planning	**60**
3.1 Strategic Quality Planning Process...........................35	
3.2 Quality Goals and Plans......................................25	
4.0 Human Resource Utilization	**150**
4.1 Human Resource Management....................................20	
4.2 Employee Involvement...40	
4.3 Quality Education and Training...............................40	
4.4 Employee Recognition and Performance Measurement............25	
4.5 Employee Well-Being and Morale..............................25	
5.0 Quality Assurance of Products and Services	**140**
5.1 Design and Introduction of Quality Products and Services.....35	
5.2 Process Quality Control......................................20	
5.3 Continuous Improvement of Processes..........................20	
5.4 Quality Assessment...15	
5.5 Documentation..10	
5.6 Business Process and Support Service Quality.................20	
5.7 Supplier Quality...20	
6.0 Quality Results	**180**
6.1 Product and Service Quality Results..........................90	
6.2 Business Process, Operational, and Support Service Quality Results......................................50	
6.3 Supplier Quality Results.....................................40	
7.0 Customer Satisfaction	**300**
7.1 Determining Customer Requirements and Expectations..........30	
7.2 Customer Relationship Management.............................50	
7.3 Customer Service Standards...................................20	
7.4 Commitment to Customers......................................15	
7.5 Complaint Resolution for Quality Improvement................25	
7.6 Determining Customer Satisfaction............................20	
7.7 Customer Satisfaction Results................................70	
7.8 Customer Satisfaction Comparison.............................70	
TOTAL POINTS	1000

Source: U.S. Dept. of Commerce, 1991 Application Guidelines, National Quality Award, p. 5.

Many potential consumers are not aware of the advantages and uses of the products. If a company is not aware of consumer requirements and expectations, it should survey its potential publics. Companies also need to constantly plan for future customers. One way to do this is to give consideration to the development of future economic and sociological trends, examining the challenges and opportunities they present for business.

Think, for example, what the women's movement and two-career families have done for demand for such products as disposable diapers, take-out food, no-iron clothing, and video entertainment. Companies need to ask what other trends are out there on the horizon, waiting to reshape the business scene. Being the first to spot, and plan for, these trends may put a firm way ahead of the crowd.

Stress current (or future) themes that appeal to the consumer of today (or tomorrow), rather than the consumer of yesteryear. Since it takes time to plan advertising campaigns, this means that "staying ahead of the game" is absolutely necessary. Regarding consumer choices, predicting future trends, rather than simply determining current trends, becomes the order of the day.

A good example of such action was recently provided by the Leo Burnett agency in its research on behalf of McDonald's. According to Bernice Kanner (1990: 16), the agency hired futurist John Naisbitt to pinpoint some major consumer trends and it assigned a team to study other visionaries' predictions of consumer attitudes. They zeroed in on three common beliefs: "Americans had been out-slicked and out-advertised so long that they were hungry to return to basic human values; as society becomes increasingly high tech, there's a need for a 'high-touch' antidote; and the expression of individuality is more important than the status associated with designer clothes." Another trend that McDonald's has spotted is the health interests, which has resulted in their new low-calorie McLean burger.

CUSTOMER RELATIONSHIP MANAGEMENT

The second Baldrige requirement in the consumer satisfaction area is customer relationship management. This area is worth 1/6 of the three hundred total points for customer satisfaction. According to the guidelines for applications, the company must first of all ensure easy access for customers to seek assistance and to comment. This might include telephone, personal, and written messages. Second, the company must describe followup with customers on products to determine satisfaction with transactions and to seek data for improvement. Third, a description of the selection, training, improvement, attitude and morale determination, and recognition and rewards for customer contact personnel must be addressed. Then the company must consider the technology and logistic support that customer contact personnel can use to provide good service. This might include information systems, followup files, and tickler systems. Next, the customer relationship management aspect of the award considers how the company analyzes key customer-related data and information to assess costs and market consequences for policy development, planning, and resource allocation.

Finally, companies must find ways to evaluate customer relationship management. This would include response accuracy, timeliness, and customer satisfaction with contacts. The evaluations should then be used to improve training, technology, or customer-oriented management processes.

CUSTOMER SERVICE STANDARDS

The third criterion is customer service standards, which is worth twenty points out of three hundred. The company must describe its customer standards and tell how they keep these standards effective and timely. How do they track, evaluate, and improve these standards? They could measure response time, problem resolution time, accuracy, and completeness.

COMMITMENT TO CUSTOMERS

Commitment to customers is the fourth criterion, and it is worth fifteen points. The company should set up a list of commitments to promote trust in its products, services, and relationships. The company must tell how it addresses principal concerns of customers, and tell whether these commitments are clear and unequivocal so that they do not weaken consumer trust.

COMPLAINT RESOLUTION

In the fifth position on the Baldrige list for consumer satis-faction is complaint resolution for quality improvement. The company must describe "how it handles complaints, resolves them and uses complaint information for quality improvement and for presentation of the recurrence of problems." These evaluations include trends in response time and trends in percent of cases resolved on the first contact.

These complaints can then be analyzed by the company and translated into improvements in processes, service standards, and information to customers to help them use the products more effectively. The complaints can also provide insights for better training of customer contact personnel.

One simple way to address complaints is to make it company policy to apologize for poor service. According to Cynthia Cros-sen (1990: B1, B3), "apologies have all but disappeared from America's commercial discourse. This cannot help but annoy consumers; it's bad enough to be inconvenienced, but it's worse not to even have an acknowledgment of this fact from the firm." According to Crossen, "In some cases, the expression of quick and sincere regrets could prevent a letter-writing campaign, an insurance claim or even a lawsuit. Yet many people on the front lines of service won't give their customers the peculiar satisfaction of hearing someone accept blame while expressing sympathy—all conveyed by the simple words 'I'm sorry.' " Some planning, development of corporate policy, and communication of that policy via training programs could prevent this.

DEVELOPING METHODS OF DETERMINING CONSUMER SATISFACTION

In step 6 the award specifies that the company should have methods of determining what the level of consumer satisfaction is. They must also show how satisfaction information is used in quality improvement and how they are improving their methods for determining customer satisfaction.

Exhibit 7.1
Areas to Address in Determining Consumer Satisfaction

a. how the company determines customer satisfaction for customer groups.

Address: (1) brief description of market segments and customer groups;

and (2) the process for determining customer satisfaction for customer

groups. Include what information is sought, frequency of surveys, inter-

views or other contacts, and how objectivity is assured. Describe how the

company sets the customer satisfaction measurement scale to adequately

capture key information that accurately reflects customer preference.

b. how customer satisfaction relative to competitors is determined.

c. how customer satisfaction data are analyzed and compared with other cus-

tomer satisfaction indicators such as complaints and gains and losses of

customers. Describe how such comparisons are used to improve customer

satisfaction determination.

d. how the company evaluates and improves its overall methods and measurement

scales used in determining customer satisfaction and customer satisfaction

relative to competitors.

Notes:

(1) Information sought in determining customer satisfaction may include spe-

cific product and service features and the relative importance of these

features to customers, thus supplementing information sought in deter-

mining customer requirements and expectations.

(2) The customer satisfaction measurement scale may include both numerical

designators and the descriptors assigned to them. An effective scale is

one that provides the company with accurate information about specific

product and service features and about the customers' likely market

behaviors.

Source: U.S. Department of Commerce, 1991 Application Guidelines, National
        Quality Award, p. 19.

Some specific suggestions offered in the Baldrige proposal
guidelines to determine the level of consumer satisfaction are
developed in exhibit 7.1.

We have viewed the Baldrige guidelines for general methods
of determining customer satisfaction. Recent media interviews

with PR specialists and CEOs point to some specific actions a firm might take. Once you have identified customers and sent messages to these audiences, you should check how the messages were received and how your product or service was received. In Chapter 9, where we discuss evaluating your identity and image presentation, we will present a number of methods that a company can use to check how their products and services are viewed.

CONSUMER SATISFACTION RESULTS

The next-to-the-last aspect to be evaluated in the consumer satisfaction area of the Baldrige award applications is the category of consumer satisfaction results. This information is worth seventy points out of the three hundred allocated to consumer satisfaction. This type of measurement is very difficult to do. The guidebook suggests that the company measure trends and current level of indicators of consumer satisfaction for products and services. These may be segmented by customer groups if appropriate. This type of measurement would probably require results of a survey or studies by independent organizations because most of the feedback coming to companies would be adverse comments deriving from complaints about products. Consumers who like products seldom bother to call the company and compliment the product. The *Fortune* reputation surveys measure opinions of the quality of products and services but this is only done for large companies. Occasionally, surveys of product quality are done for smaller companies (*Forbes*).

There are also consumer groups that do this type of research on products or services. Consumer Reports publishes an annual auto issue in the spring of every year that reports on the results of its surveys of auto users with regard to satisfaction and repair records, its road tests of individual car models, its track tests of different car models, and its laboratory studies of the features of cars.

Every year they buy three dozen new cars from local dealers. The cars are then taken to an auto test facility, where they are thoroughly inspected for fifty items such as mechanical components, instruments and controls, fit, and finish. Defects like improperly inflated tires and loose electrical connections are noted. During this time engineers and technicians drive the cars for commuting, shopping, and other errands for at least two thousand miles to "break in the cars." They record their impressions in a log book kept in the car. After the cars are "broken in," the front end is realigned, tuning and adjustments take place, and the car is ready for a 150-mile formal test. During this test checks are made on engine and transmission, fuel economy, handling, ride, noise, seating, and climate control. Finally, such items as safety features, trunk size and design, and ability of bumpers to absorb impacts are tested. Numerical scores are attached to each item on a five-point scale ranging from poor to excellent.

In addition to tests of models another very important way to derive product information is to ask consumers how they feel about a product. This is an especially good technique to evaluate satisfaction with durables with which consumers have had an opportunity to have a number of years of experience. The most crucial question is, "Would you buy that product again?" This often takes time to assess. For example, in the April 1991 issue of *Consumer Reports* when 200 models (covering some 374,000 cars, trucks, and vans) were evaluated, 94 percent owning a 1990 car said they would buy it again, 89 percent owning a 1989 car would buy the same make and model again; for owners of 1988 models the score dropped to 86 percent. Thus consumer satisfaction needs to be studied not only immediately but over a period of time. Remember the L. L. Bean policy mentioned in Chapter 5, that you really can't evaluate the quality of the product till after it has worn out.

Consumers Union also reports on frequency of repair records. Consumer experience with 800,000 cars from 1985 to 1990 is reported using a five-point scale by car model and model year for seventeen items such as air conditioning, brakes, clutch, and transmission. To summarize these features, an overall trouble index (total number of repairs) and cost index (average cost of repair and maintenance) is reported for each model.

While these extensive reliability reports are available for the automobile industry, they may not be available in many other industries. Companies that want this type of feedback may have to turn to their industry association or to private testing groups. Sometimes a company's warranty files can be used to derive a sample for a consumer satisfaction study. In any event these studies can make vital contributions to product improvement and hence, to reputation for quality. Even companies that are not applying for a Baldrige Award might do well to explore these assessments of their product quality.

The guidelines for the awards also specify that the company study trends and current levels in major adverse indicators. Adverse indicators include complaints, claims, refunds, recalls, returns, repeat services, litigation, replacements, downgrades, repairs, warranty costs and warranty work, and sanctions received under regulation or contract. Obviously, a company is more likely to receive criticism than plaudits from its customers. How many consumers send a note to thank a company for an excellent product? Yet, they will tell their friends and often these personal recommendations will result in new sales. Perhaps it would be good company policy to send annual questionnaires to people in its warranty files to see what they think of the product and hence, what their reputation for quality is. In this way, they would get good as well as bad feedback. Survey research studies of response show that one is more likely to get response from those who are very interested in the product. Thus, it is likely that people who are very angry with the product or who are very pleased with it will be more likely to respond than those who feel that it is so-so.

COMPARISON OF SATISFACTION RATINGS WITH THOSE OF COMPETITORS

The final consumer satisfaction criterion is a comparison of consumer satisfaction results with those of competitors. This comparison is worth seventy points or 22.5 percent of all the consumer satisfaction scores. The Baldrige guidelines suggest that the following areas be addressed:

- Comparison of customer satisfaction results. Such comparisons should be made with principal competitors in the company's key markets, industry averages, industry leaders, and world leaders.
- Surveys, competitive awards, recognition, and ratings by independent organizations, including customers. Briefly describe surveys, awards, recognition, and ratings. Include how quality and quality attributes are considered as factors in the evaluations of these independent organizations.
- Trends in gaining or losing customers and in customer and customer account retention. Briefly summarize gains and losses of customers, including those gained from or lost to competitors. Address customer groups or market segments, as appropriate.
- Trends in gaining and losing market share relative to major competitors, domestic and foreign. Briefly explain significant changes in terms of quality comparisons and quality trends.

Measurement of consumer satisfaction is often done by consumer organizations. Interesting results can be obtained by comparing reliability over the years. A recent article of *Consumer Reports* (April 1991: 248–249), studied results for cars that were five years old when their owners were surveyed (so that the owners had a long opportunity to observe the car's performance). Looking at the changes from 1980 to 1990 in terms of problems per one hundred cars, the number of problems for American cars—Chrysler, GM, and Ford—has fallen by approximately 30 percent. Nevertheless, it has fallen for the three key Japanese producers—Nissan, Toyota and Honda—who also experienced a drop of approximately 1/3 in problems so that they are still above the American producers in terms of reliability; that is, they have fewer problems and thus are more reliable. These comparisons, while painful, are necessary for companies to conduct in order to find out how they "stack up."

Now that mechanical bugs are gradually ironed out of the cars so that they have a very good reliability rate, there will be a new emphasis on customer service ratings as a method to compete. Analyst Maryann N. Keller, vice president at Furman, Selz, Mager, Dietz and Birney says, "The nature of a customer is changing . . . it's no longer a customer over one event; it's a customer over the life of the car." (*Dallas Morning News*, March 24, 1991, p. 1)

Auto dealers are revamping their training and hiring practices. Another tactic to improve service is to interview the buyer. When luxury buyers were interviewed (Kunde 1991), they claimed that what they disliked most was buying the car. They complained about the way they were treated (*Dallas Morning News*, March 24, 1991, p. 10H). The employees of the Infiniti dealers are sent to Scottsboro for training that includes two days of track testing under the tutelage of professional race car drivers. The employees take turns on a slalom course at 30, 40, and 50 mph. "The idea is to get sales and dealership personnel both enthusiastic and knowledgeable about their products. Salesmen are encouraged to use 'soft sell,' courteous approaches. Dealership design is carefully crafted to be softly lit and spacious." For years the service department was ignored because warranty work was a money loser. As Maryann Keller says, "Dealers are recognizing that service is important, not only as a profit center, but as a continuing link between someone who bought and will buy in the future. It's dawning on everyone." Some dealerships feature a window where customers can see their car being serviced and can walk in freely and talk to a technician.

Another problem in the service area was that most customers pick up their car at the same time at the end of the day. Now sales personnel double as lot assistants, moving cars during peak times. This also builds teams among dealership employees.

Another approach to improve dealership relations is a new hiring method. Barry Pryor, president of Sewell Lexus in Dallas, says, "We are getting people right out of college who want a career in the car business. They come into the dealership as service advisers and can later move through sales." Thus, before a person is sent to do a relatively high "pay-back job" like sales, a thorough understanding of what people want in a product and how the business works can be relayed. The new employee starts to build a career in the business.

The Japanese, too, are trying to improve their service according to James Womack, senior research associate at the Massachusetts Institute of Technology (Kunde, 1991: 10H). Their idea is that the cheapest sale is the repeat sale. Thus, as products improve, the new tie-breakers for sales will be service. Hence, the top area to build a corporate reputation and differentiate one's company from other companies in the 1990s will be service.

CHAPTER 8

Financial Soundness and Corporation Reputation

Financial soundness is an important determinant of corporate reputation. As mentioned previously, it is one of the eight determinants considered in the *Fortune* reputation surveys. In our surveys, the public relations specialists rank it as third (out of eight) in importance, while the CEOs rank it fifth (see table 5.1). But the causality runs both ways. Not only does financial soundness help to "cause" a good reputation; in addition, a good reputation can help to "cause" financial soundness. This is because firms with good reputations, enjoying the confidence of the public, will find it easier to raise funds (both debt and equity) to support their activities.

In chapter 5 we observed that good reputation can help the company in four areas—labor, finance, sales, and community relations. The finance area covers five aspects:

- Ability to float more loans
- Lower interest rate on loans

- Less restriction on selling bonds
- Ability to issue stock at higher prices
- Ability to sell more stock

Of these five, the ability to sell more stock was rated first by both the public relations specialists and CEOs we polled. This makes sense, because this ability assures the firm that there will be a constantly full pool of capital to support the firm's present and future needs. After all, no matter how creative, service-oriented, innovative, and efficient a firm may be, if it does not have the continuing financial resources to support its operations, then it has no long-term future.

In too many circles, financial matters may be thought of as strictly the province of finance professionals; but this is definitely not the case. We have repeatedly made the point that it is not really the facts, but instead the *perception* of the facts, that determines corporate reputation. Nowhere is this more true than in the field of finance. Investors and creditors risk their money in anticipation of future results. What happened in the past (income, dividends, capital gains, etc.) is informative only in that it may help to predict the future. But, by themselves, past results (whether they be positive or negative) have no value. What is important is the interpretation of the corporation's financial report card. Financial people may be extremely skilled at producing this report card but may not always do a good job of interpreting it.

Finance professionals within the firm have a dual task: keeping the firm financially sound and convincing the investing public that the firm is financially sound! In this latter task, they will be assisted by management and public relations specialists who pave the way for good communication with the public. According to Mike Devaney (1991: 158), "The argument against the finance specialist as corporate leader usually centers on their 'lack of corporate skill' or their failure to recognize that the 'numbers often lie.' " If finance people are "deficient" in this regard, then the firm has to take steps to see that there is a communication "bridge" between the corporate finance people and the investing public. Without such a bridge, good news may be garbled and misinterpreted; bad news may take on the worst possible connotation.

A lot of happenings in the market may be beyond the control of an individual company; but the public needs to be convinced that management has the ability and confidence to cope with whatever risks are thrown in its direction. If the finance people have difficulty in getting this message across in a nontechnical manner, then they need to seek help from public relations specialists and/or image consultants. The stock price mirrors the investing public's evaluation. A firm's stock price is important, not only because it indicates how much the firm can get for its shares in a stock offering (there may not even be a stock offering planned in the firm's short-term future), but also because it is looked upon as a barometer of success by suppliers, customers, and present and potential suppliers of capital (creditors and investors).

There are signs that finance is an increasingly important field of endeavor, with the skills of finance personnel more highly regarded now than they have been in the past. This is probably a reflection of the fact that financial restructurings and packagings in the market have become increasingly complicated. There is no room for novices. Ida Picker (1989: 47) states that "quite a few people applaud the perked-up status of what was once the lowly bean counter. Recruiters report a growing trend of grooming chief financial officers for the top spot, with some headhunters estimating that nearly 25 percent of top corporate leaders are former CFOs, about twice as many as in 1960." As more and more CFOs become CEOs, the connection between corporate reputation and financial soundness is strengthened. The communication skills of finance people become increasingly important as more of them inspire to the very top leadership spots in corporate America.

In ordinary times, when markets are good and the firm is profitable, finance professionals may have a relatively easy (although still challenging) task to convince "the world" that the firm has a good reputation. When times are bad—recession, product tampering, overall service complaints, financial difficulties—the task is that much more difficult.

RECOMMENDATIONS FOR THE GOOD TIMES ... AND THE BAD

Research your company, your policies, and your competitors' activities before you hire consultants. Finance professionals should always be informed about the *Fortune* reputation surveys. These surveys indicate that consistently good performance is really essential for a good reputation. These *Fortune* surveys contain important information—even for firms too small to be included. They give a general idea of trends; one can compare, over time, the relative performance of different industry groups and the eight criteria for good reputation. The nuances of investor moods are revealed; one can plot the rise and fall in reputation of various firms and ponder the reasons "why." Also, there are always very interesting accompanying articles giving the views on corporate reputation of numerous executives, most of whom are very successful at maintaining good corporate reputation.

Financial journals—both academic- and practitioner-oriented— often have articles related (either directly or indirectly) to corporate reputation; the financial staff should make use of such information. If a specific project is being planned, it might be good to do some basic, very preliminary research before you hire and pay consultants to do anything. Public libraries and libraries in trade associations often provide inexpensive or free computerized searching for the latest information on just about any topic. Sometimes it may be more effective to do some "spadework" before you go to the experts. Only those businesses knowing nothing about availability of public information would be foolish enough to rush to an expert before considering information that is "free."

For example, if you were contemplating changing your firm's name, why not spend some time looking at the results reported by other firms who have done just that? A computerized search could provide abstracts of some articles written on this topic, reporting the results experienced by other firms. An article such as "The Valuation Effects of Corporate Name Changes" (by Jean-Claude Bosch and Mark Hirschey in *Financial Management* [Winter 1989]) would most likely come up in a search. Having studied the stock return behavior of firms that change their names, the authors report that (p. 72) "On an overall basis, it can be concluded that the valuation effects of name changes are only modest and transitory." This information would not, of course, put an end to further consideration of a name change. But it is good to get such basic information before you even think about hiring an expert to advise about the name change. And, when faced with that hiring decision, it might be helpful to do another search about the prospective candidates and their recent successes and failures. In the information age, it just does not make sense to hire outsiders without doing some independent research on the "history" of these outsiders. This does not mean that you make the decision based solely on past performance; but it does mean that you have better input for making the decision about your future.

It would seem that there are numerous candidates to handle this library assignment: a secretary or administrative assistant eager to have personal talents "stretched," the firm's librarian, management trainees who profit from having the experience of varied assignments. Asking your own employees for assistance in researching ways to improve the firm's reputation may have a positive effect on morale. Motivated employees are an important building block for a good reputation. One way to keep employees motivated is to provide a work environment in which employees can constantly grow and extend themselves and tackle a variety of tasks.

It is not an imposition to ask employees in the finance area to read the most current publications and to search for information related specifically to the firm's current plans. This can be presented as a challenging and very interesting assignment. Most of us are happiest when we are encouraged to stay current in our fields and function at the highest level of our intellectual capacity.

Cultivate good relationships with your shareholders. Another important recommendation in the financial area is to cultivate good relationships with owners. The corporate press is filled with reports of owner-manager disagreements—disagreements that do not always end happily. These two groups need to get along better, for the benefit of both. Outsiders may reason that if the firm cannot even please its owners, how can it please anybody else? Both owners and managers may end up suffering as a result of disagreements publicly aired. Corporate governance is an important issue for the 1990s, and firms need to deal with it properly.

Shareholders are putting pressure on managers; and, in many cases, they are achieving the results they seek. James A. White (1991: C1) recently reported that

The solid wall of corporate opposition to shareholder-rights proxy measures is beginning to crumble, as big pension funds acquire concessions from an unprecedented number of large companies.

Eager to avoid disruptive proxy contests during the annual meeting season, 25 companies have given ground by accepting corporate governance measures in recent months. . . .

The growing concessions have been won by a slowly maturing shareholders-rights movement, led by public pension funds from California and a handful of big cities and states and by the activist United Shareholders Association.

Corporate governance has become important enough to be a major determinant of corporate reputation. It is coming to the point that some shareholders, especially large institutional investors, are unwilling to accept situations in which shareholder rights are not acknowledged and respected. The United Shareholders Association, using corporate governance data published by the Washington, D.C.–based Investor Responsibility Research Center, recently published a list of the ten firms achieving best shareholder rights. The list is composed of the following companies:

Bear Stearns

Valhi

American Electric Power

Autodesk

Connor Peripherals

L. A. Gear

Price Company

Silicon Graphics

Texas Utilities

WD-40

This is only one small portion of the "1991 Shareholder 1000," the third annual evaluation of corporate responsiveness to shareholders—an evaluation done by the United Shareholders Association.

As studies such as this one become more numerous and better publicized, corporations will be even more hard pressed to pay close attention to corporate governance issues. There is no choice about this. Companies that do not respond will find themselves unable to compete for funds in capital markets.

Unfortunately, there are firms that just have not gotten this message yet. Or, if they got the message, they are refusing to act on it. A recent example of this was the May 1991 shareholder meeting of General Motors Corp., a meeting in which shareholders were asked to vote on a plan to boost executive pensions. Although the GM shareholders approved the plan by a vote of 83 percent to 17 percent, the proposal attracted much antimanagement sentiment. This was an issue that could have been settled by GM's board, yet management had made the decision to bring it to shareholder vote. The result was a lot of unfavorable publicity—publicity only fueled by the comments of Chair Roger B. Smith: "It's an experiment in corporate governance that's gone astray. . . . If this is something that gets blown out of proportion by the press and damages our reputation, it doesn't help us" (White 1990: A3). This comment only made the situation worse, seemingly dealing a blow to corporate governance advocates. It does seem logical that GM shareholders should be able to vote on management compensation; after all, it is *their* company.

Another "blooper" in the corporate governance arena was recently provided by Sears, Roebuck & Co. Faced with the possibility of having corporate governance advocate Robert A. G. Monks elected to its board of directors, Sears took the surprising step of announcing that it would shrink the size of its board from fifteen to ten members. Leslie Wayne (1991: D2) reported that a Sears spokesperson (David Shute, general counsel) said the company had long been considering trimming its board but advanced its timetable: "We did move ahead on our timetable to make it more difficult for Mr. Monks. . . . he's not the kind of director needed. His agenda and his interest is in corporate governance and . . . we really need our directors to focus primarily on financial performance. We regard governance issues as a distraction."

Statements such as this cannot help but enrage investors, and this is certainly an unwise thing to do. Why make statements that deliberately infuriate investors? Why bite the hand that feeds you? Firms must be aware of current economic and sociological trends. Corporate governance is definitely one of these trends; speaking out against it will not make it go away. A company concerned about its reputation should take steps to make its philosophy of corporate governance clear to its own shareholders as well as to important shareholder groups that shape the market. There are two different stands that a firm can take on the issue of corporate governance. First, make the firm more democratic by catering more closely to shareholder demands and directly allow shareholders more of a voice in governing the firm. Second, suggest that the best way to serve shareholders is to earn them an above-average return on their money. Maybe this can be done most effectively by allowing managers freedom to do the task for which they were hired. An extremely active style of corporate governance could have negative effects and end up weakening corporations, rather than strengthening them. Corporate performance could be worse, rather than better; managers might find themselves so busy reporting to, and pleasing, active investors that they would not have enough time to deal with the challenges presented by competitors, suppliers, and customers.

Modern economies have been built on the principle of specialization of work, with each participant becoming an expert in one, rather than many, fields of endeavor. The image of the modern-day corporation is one in which each individual has a job to do and is left to do that job with independence and a minimum amount of direction from those above. According to John F. Welch, Jr., CEO of General Electric, "If we are to get the reflexes and speed we need, we've got to simplify and delegate more—simply trust more. We need to drive self-confidence deep into the organization. A company can't distribute self-confidence, but it can foster it by removing layers and giving people a chance to win" (1990: 30).

Delegation has to begin at the very top, with investors making basic delegations to managers. One cannot help but wonder if a firm with excessively active investors can set the proper tone. Will executives have the freedom and self-confidence to make the bold moves necessary for success in today's markets? More important, can they create the kind of atmosphere in which people at all levels of the organization feel supported?

Which of the two philosophies described above "fits" the particular firm is a decision that must be made on an individual basis. The important point is that the firm face the issue of corporate governance head on and deal with it in a reasonable, well-planned fashion. Avoidance and/or inflammatory comments are tactics that simply will not work!

Even in bad times, keep your company reputation in the public eye. An important part of the job of finance practitioners is to plan for and cope with bad times. And they have to be good at communicating the fact that planning for the future, as well as dealing with the present, is part of their job. Knowing the individualized needs of the firm may dictate an unusual stance, where a firm must travel in a direction that is different from the rest of the crowd. For example, making use of a high proportion of debt relative to equity became popular in the 1980s; yet for some firms this proved to be a recipe for disaster. John R. Dorfman (1991: C1) recently commented:

Remember how analysts used to mock low-debt companies as "underleveraged"?

You heard that kind of talk a lot in the 1980s, but you don't hear much of it now. Companies with little or no debt on their balance sheets are sitting pretty now that recession has arrived.

Debt-free or low-debt companies stand a greater chance of weathering the recessionary storm. They can buy stores, factories, equipment or whole divisions from cash-strapped competitors. If push comes to shove, they still have the ability to borrow money—something their rivals may no longer be able to do.

The important message here is that whatever financial structure the firm has decided upon, it must take the initiative to present itself favorably to the media and actively choose the vocabulary that seems appropriate, rather than passively accept the descriptive vocabulary chosen by the media or other onlookers. Choices of words can subtly (or not so subtly) affect perceptions. For example, finance practitioners in a low-debt company need to stress the low-risk aspect of the firm, that is, sell the fact that "here's a financial structure that can be supportive in bad times and in good." Likewise, finance practitioners in a high-risk firm need to stress that the firm can be a "high flyer" when times are good but can also survive when times are bad. Others within the firm (advertising and public relations personnel, for example) should be able to assist in the delivery of the correct message to the media.

Unfortunately, when times are bad, there may not be enough public relations and other personnel to support the finance group in communicating with the investing public. As firms feel the "pinch," they may make poor expenditure cutting decisions. Thomas Garbett, author of *How to Build a Corporation's Identity and Project Its Image* (1988), has studied how firms have handled advertising during a recession and what has happened as a result of cut-back policies.

Studies by agencies such as Meldrum & Fewsmith, Inc., and the McGraw-Hill Research Group (Garbett 1988: 234) have shown that companies that continue to advertise during recessionary periods survive them better. "Analysis of six hundred industrial companies, showed that business-to-business firms that maintained or increased their advertising expenditures during the 1981–82 recession averaged significantly higher sales growth both during the recession and in the following three years than did those that eliminated or decreased advertising" (Garbett 1988:237). In a recession, companies may change the orientation of their ads as Garbett points out: "In the 1980–82 recession, Michelin switched from saying that its steel-belted radial tires were expensive but worth it, and instead stressed how 'surprisingly affordable Michelins were.' "

The patterns of advertising changes observed by Garbett show that advertising addressed to the financial community to enhance stock value tends to drop off during a recession. Softer institutional-like advertising that expounds philosophies also tends to decrease. Sales-related corporate ads may increase, except that the weaker products may not be supported by ads.

In a period when customers may not be able to buy because of financial difficulties or because of product shortages, it may be wiser to use advertising that enhances the quality image and reputation of the company. This type of advertising may be better than ads that try to promote sales by price cuts in a nonbuying atmosphere. These ads may tend to cheapen the image of the product and not appreciably increase sales.

Often firms are forced to cut their corporate and product ads because stockholder dividends have been cut and workers have been laid off. The company must then show that it has an austerity program throughout all of its departments. The results of these cuts in corporate advertising show that favorable awareness of the company drops rapidly. How long this memory decay will take depends on the company. If the company name is not well known or it has recently changed, the memory decay can be very rapid.

In short, a fairly new company should maintain at least some level of corporate image building and advertising even during a recessionary period. It may be tempting to cut this spending, but that is probably not a wise move. In addition, cuts in advertising to the financial community can have disastrous consequences in both the short- and long-term future. Bad press in the financial community can affect stock prices, bond ratings, and consumer confidence levels for many years to come.

Respond to bad news immediately and confidently. A recession is a "bad" event with which an entire economy has to deal. Finance practitioners also have to be concerned with "bad" events that are specific to the firm and to mitigate, as much as possible, the negative effects of such events.

An important recommendation that emerged in our research is to deal with bad news immediately and confidently. Done well, such action can end up enhancing the reputation of the firm. Probably the best example of this in recent memory is the manner in which J&J handled the Tylenol scare, which resulted in the deaths of seven people in Chicago in 1982. The company's response was quick and authoritative, although costly in monetary terms. But the company was able to sustain the support of its many customers and generally emerged quite unscathed from the incident. Exxon's response to the Valdez oil spill was quite different and the company suffered for the way it handled the problem.

Rumors and rumblings can affect corporate reputation, whether there is a basis in fact or not. This was brought home recently in the irate letter sent to the *Wall Street Journal* by William L. Gladstone and Ray J. Groves, co-chief executives of Ernst & Young, protesting the article written on the possible bankruptcy of Ernst & Young. Strongly denying that the rumor had any basis in fact, Gladstone and Groves wrote: "Fortunately for our 23,000 people and thousands of clients, Ernst & Young is strong enough to withstand this kind of publicity" (1990: A19). Putting aside for the moment an opinion on the accuracy of this particular rumor, this comment has a more general application. What about firms that are not strong enough (or smart enough) to withstand negative publicity that happens to be untrue? It is frightening to contemplate the far-reaching and long-term effects of rumor power.

It must be remembered that reputation is a perception, not necessarily a fact. If firms leave the market "hanging," much anxiety may be created in the minds of investors and this can adversely affect corporate reputation. Telling investors the bad news may actually be a better strategy than letting them imagine what the bad news may be; they may imagine things being worse than they actually are. Generalized anxiety may have a worse effect on the market than the actual bad news, which has the virtue of at least being limited and definite. Investors may feel more confident knowing about the bad news as well as the strategy the firm plans to employ to cope with it.

According to a recent article in the *Institutional Investor*, "A company should be open to the investment community and go out of its way to regularly bring together analysts and top brass. It should make sure that followers' expectations approach reality, so there are no surprises. It should quickly and candidly address rumors, news and unfolding developments. It should not stick its head in the sand during lean times" (1989: 58). This article is interesting in that it reports on a survey to highlight especially good investor relations programs. Ten firms were selected as the "cream of the crop" and are profiled in detail.

On the other side of the coin, Pfizer has been cited in the press recently for poor investor relations. Pfizer was perceived as slow to comment on a congressional investigation chaired by John Dingell, regarding defects in the Shiley heart valve manufactured by a subsidiary of Pfizer. What is interesting is that "the Dingell hearing yielded little that the financial community didn't already know about the Shiley controversy. It was, to put it bluntly, a non-event. Nevertheless, considerable damage was done. And Pfizer, which could have been reveling in its new products, found itself confronting an investor relations crisis" (Faber 1990: 189).

Develop a crisis control center. Most firms will face crises arising in a number of directions. Experts agree that it is good practice to develop a crisis control center with a crisis plan. This decade's scare is the environmental crisis. Society is increasingly sensitive to environmental issues. New technology makes it easier to detect and measure pollutants, accidents, and other dangers. Firms will have to develop new ways to deal with these problems. Food and pharmaceutical companies have had to deal with tampering problems through more effective packaging and labeling. Oil companies have had to deal with oil spills and chemical companies have to cope with pollution and threats of explosion. How companies handle themselves in a crisis situation is crucial to their reputation. Corporations need to plan in advance for strategies to handle adverse situations. Just as many companies have a "calling tree" for snow days or other emergencies, the company should envision possible emergencies and draw up lists of people who should be contacted. These lists might include the CEO, plant manager, different supervisors, the company lawyer, and the public relations staff. A second list might include people in the community who might be helpful, such as local government officials, favorably inclined newspaper reporters, research laboratories, and consultants. Possibly government agencies should be listed too. Lists should include home addresses and phone numbers, as well as office numbers so that people can be contacted in the evening and on weekends.

Stan Sauerhaft and Chris Atkins (1989: 194) have also suggested a "crises command center" with checklists for staffing (management, secretaries, and couriers) and equipment (word processors, facsimile transmitters, tape recorder-equipped telephones). Possibly, too, some emergency drills might be tried to be sure that swift action will be taken when needed.

We have discussed advance planning. There are several suggestions, gleaned from publications on the treatment of crisis problems. Sauerhaft and Atkins suggest that a company be as cooperative and candid as possible. It should also show concern and take actions to find a solution to the problem. It may also have to make its own investigation. If a company does make an investigation, it should hire an outside consultant with excellent credentials. That is why so many firms, for example, hire the "big six" accounting firms to audit their financial statements. The employers are hoping that some of the prestige of the auditing company will "rub off" on their firms.

At the same time, however, it is absolutely essential to have a CEO who is visible, especially in times of crisis. This did not happen with Exxon at the time of the Alaska oil spill, and it was unfortunate. The public needs to see, *deserves* to see, that control is there and being exercised. In a later interview (*Time*, March 25, 1990), one year after the Alaska spill, Exxon's chair, Lawrence Rawl, defended his action of failing to rush to the scene of the event by saying that, "We had concluded that there was simply too much for me to coordinate from New York." In terms of the loss of public good will and corporate reputation, it would seem that Rawl paid dearly for this decision. As John F. Budd, Jr. (1990: A12) has stated: "One lesson the 1980s should have taught American business leaders is the pivotal importance of corporate credibility. Achieving it, sustaining it, protecting it is not a damage control matter. It has to be a daily activity. It demands visible, candid even visionary leadership."

CONCLUDING REMARKS

In chapter 3, we discussed the fact that the academic literature does show some connection between financial variables and corporate reputation; but it is a connection that appears to be tenuous at best. This means that finance practitioners must recognize, and act upon, the fact that financial variables, although important, are not the only determinants of corporate reputation.

Those who evaluate corporate reputation are interested in nonfinancial as well as financial variables. Thus, finance practitioners within a firm show that they are true professionals when they practice their craft in concert with managers and public relations specialists, so that the outside world sees a picture of organized, united, and confident use of capital resources. Finance practitioners attempting to work in isolation will self-destruct.

Building and maintaining the financial soundness of the firm is a major part of the finance practitioner's job. Seeing that the public (customers, suppliers, investors, creditors, etc.) is convinced of the financial soundness of the firm is the other, sometimes neglected, part of the job of finance professionals. Without this, the firm can never build for itself a consistently favorable corporate reputation.

CHAPTER 9

Corporate Identity, Corporate Visibility, and Reputation in the Community

According to Socrates, "The way to gain a good reputation is to endeavor to be what you desire to appear." Establishing a corporate identity requires both strategic planning and proactive behavior.

As evidenced by our survey, both CEOs and public relations specialists find establishing identity in the marketplace a very crucial step in building a good corporate reputation. Much of what both groups learned about their corporate image and identity came from "word of mouth" methods. Although this is a major concern of the 1990s, it dates back to ancient times. Writings from ancient India address the king's spies whose functions, in addition to espionage, included keeping the king in touch with public opinion, championing the king in public, and spreading rumors favorable to the government (Cutlip, Center, and Broom 1985: 23). The origin of the word "propaganda" dates back to the seventeenth century, when the Catholic Church set up its *congregatio de propaganda* (congregation for propagating the faith).

The former American Telephone and Telegraph Company was not only a pioneer in the communications industry, but they were also innovators in establishing their corporate identity program. In 1912, they established a public relations bureau that, in addition to responsibilities associated with information dissemination, tracked trends in public opinion (Cutlip, Center, and Broom 1985: 38). Although the processes for establishing identity and reevaluating who you are have changed, it still remains a crucial part of any management and marketing plan.

In chapters 5 and 6 we discussed what a good reputation can do for a firm in the community. Both the CEOs and the PR specialists highly ranked the ability to locate in better communities when a company has good corporate image. The PR specialists felt that the second most important value of a good image was the ability to obtain media coverage. The CEOs, however, felt that the ability to increase possibilities for business extensions was second in importance. Third and fourth in importance for PR specialists were ability to deal with local governments and increased possibility for business extensions. For the CEOs, ability to deal with local governments to obtain media coverage were tied for third and fourth place. Finally, the lowest rating for importance of good reputation in the community by both groups was ability to establish consumer trust.

CORPORATE IDENTITY PROGRAMS

Thus far we have not discussed the importance of establishing identity in building a good image. This identity is especially important to community relationships. Companies that succeed in establishing a good corporate image have found a definite need to "practice what they preach." Estee Lauder Company, for example, began more than six years ago exploring ways in which they could incorporate the public's concern for the environment into their product line. They tracked healthier lifestyle trends among their consumers and decided they needed to adapt who they were to meet what their clients needed and expected.

In early 1990, Estee Lauder launched their "Origins" cosmetics line. The line was designed with environmentally friendly ingredients and packaging, plus a built-in recycling program. The line is touted as being designed to be "harmonious with nature." Most of the line's visibility has come from word of mouth and good press. Rather than developing an extensive advertising campaign, the cosmetics line was introduced to its publics via special environmental events and joint promotions with department stores across the nation. They advertise only once a month in two publications, the Sunday *New York Times Magazine* and *L.A. Style*. Sales have exceeded the company's expectations.

William Lauder, vice president/general manager of "Origins" and grandson of company founder Estee Lauder, summarized the reasons for "Origins' "success in an April 1991 article in the *Public Relations Journal* (pp. 24–25): "We wanted to be environmentally responsible, . . . but we realized that being green (environmentally concerned) could not be our sole reason for being. What's more, we believed that simply slapping a 'now recyclable' banner on your package doesn't make you green. This green is a special sensitivity that must permeate every aspect of your marketing platform and actions." His marketing team also researched their audience enough to understand that they had high expectations of cosmetics bearing the Lauder name. The marketers focused their efforts on offering superior products and a commitment to the environment. Their researched campaign and strategy support the brand's sales and will help to further enhance the company's image.

PERSUADING PEOPLE TO RECOGNIZE THE VALUE OF IDENTITY

The success of the "Origins" campaign stresses the importance of clearly establishing the identity and purpose of your company and your product for your audience. In other words, in order to persuade your customers to buy your product or your service, they must understand and need what you are selling. Exhibit

Exhibit 9.1
Principles of Persuasion

1. <u>Identification Principle</u>

   Most people will ignore an idea, an opinion, or a point-of-view unless
   they see clearly that it affects their personal fears or desires, hopes
   or aspirations. <u>Your message must be stated in terms of the interest of</u>
   <u>your audience</u>.

2. <u>Action Principle</u>

   People seldom buy ideas separated from action -- either action taken or
   about to be taken -- by the sponsor of the idea, or action that the people
   themselves can conveniently take to prove the mint of the idea. <u>Unless a</u>
   <u>means of action is provided, people tend to shrug off appeals to do things</u>.

3. <u>Principle of Familiarity and Trust</u>

   We buy ideas only from those who we trust; we are influenced by, or adopt,
   only those opinions or points of view put forward by individuals or corporations or institutions that we regard as credible. <u>Unless the listener</u>
   <u>has confidence in the speaker, the listener is not likely to listen or to</u>
   <u>believe</u>.

4. <u>Clarity Principle</u>

   The situation must be clear to us, not confusing. The thing we observe,
   read, see, or hear, the thing that produces our impressions, must be
   clear, not subject to several interpretations. People tend to see things
   as black or white. <u>To communicate, you must employ words, symbols, or</u>
   <u>stereotypes that the receiver comprehends and responds to.</u>

<u>Effective Public Relations</u>, 6th edition, pp. 178-179, Scott M. Cutlip, Allen
H. Center and Glen M. Broom. Reprinted with permission from Prentice-Hall
Inc., Englewood Cliffs, New Jersey.

9.1 summarizes some tentative principles of persuasion based
on experimental research. These elements can serve as guides
in establishing a company and product identity.

The principles of persuasion listed in exhibit 9.1 are basic
guidelines that marketers and other strategic planners follow

in developing corporate identity programs. In the back of their minds, they understand the basic principles of marketing: you have to have something to sell and someone to sell it to in order to succeed. But in today's economy companies need to understand more about "the someone" whom they would like to buy their product or service.

When the Campbell Soup Company developed their "soup is good food" campaign, they were building off an already built identity. The "soup is good food" campaign carried more than one message. Campbell's Soup has always been "Mm! Mm! Good!" but that campaign mostly targeted those interested in taste. The "Soup is good food" campaign was stated not only in terms of those interested in taste, but it was also stated in terms of a new larger audience that is interested in nutrition.

The campaign included the action principle by developing the "Special Request" line of soups. The company said they too were concerned with nutritional and health value. Then, they put their words into action by developing a product with more appeal to their health-conscious clientele. Their "Special Request" line contains 1/3 of the salt that the regular line carries and less calories.

Through the years, the Campbell Soup Company has built trust and customer confidence. They have worked to provide a consistent quality product and to serve as a good corporate citizen. Years ago the company initiated a program to help fund equipment and supplies for the schools. School children and their families were asked to save their Campbell Soup labels. Schools and classes were in competition with each other to win various types of equipment for classrooms and gym classes. This campaign encouraged families to buy more Campbell's Soup. It also built familiarity and trust in the company, because they supported a cause that was "near and dear" to their customers.

Anyone familiar with a grocery store layout can show you where cans of soup are displayed. The company sells other products, including cookbooks, and they are all packaged in a consistent way. Campbell's Soup provides a consistent message.

It is good family food. They even offer "homestyle products," like Mom used to make, for customers who are working. Campbell's provides family food and they sponsor family events. Their message is simple: their soup is good food. As a result, it is difficult to think of store-bought soup without envisioning their red and white cans. Thus, Campbell's has used symbols that have clearly identified their products.

ESTABLISHING CORPORATE IDENTITY

The overall importance of corporate identity is indicated by Wally Olins (1990: F13), chair of Wolff Olins Ltd.:

An organization's corporate identity can inspire loyalty, shape decisions, aid recognition and attract customers. It is vital to effective employee recruitment and to the way people work together inside a company. And it is directly related to profitability. A corporation's identity, if it is perceived negatively, can work against even the best marketing innovations and strategic initiatives.

As proof that brands can have a life quite separate from that of the company, Olins cites the case of Betty Crocker. Created in 1924 for General Mills, the Crocker portrait was painted seven times—each time to suit the national mood. Olins indicates that in 1940, surveys indicated she was recognized by nine of of 10 Americans!

Another interesting example of an inviting and effective "image" was recently created by Southwest Airlines. The company painted an airplane to resemble a whale "Shamu" to announce being named as the official carrier to Sea World of Texas in San Antonio. The plane was seen in papers all over the country, providing free publicity for both the carrier and Sea World. The idea was received so well that Southwest Airlines recently painted a plane to resemble the Texas flag in tribute to its relationship with Texas.

Lawrence Ackerman (1988: 28) discusses the case of an organization struggling to differentiate itself from its competition:

Mt. Sinai Hospital in New York City recently set up a medical hot line for consumers who need guidance on locating a specialist to diagnose specific symptoms. All referrals are to Mt. Sinai–affiliated physicians. In establishing this service, Mt. Sinai is taking aggressive steps to differentiate itself from the other New York area hospitals and to build a broader patient base.

Estee Lauder's "Origins" campaign put them in front of not only their original customer base, but it also exposed them to a new audience. Those who may not have used Estee Lauder's products in the past may consider using them as an alternative because of the company's efforts to save the environment. The six years the company took to plan their campaign let them establish who they wanted to be and determine means for gaining visibility.

INCREASING CORPORATE VISIBILITY

Many firms wish to have increased visibility to their many publics. There are some tactics suggested by Stan Sauerhaft and Chris Atkins (1989) to address this problem. Three possibilities are: taking a stand on an issue, being generous, or sponsoring or associating with a popular event or cause. A 1986 study showed that CEOs of America's most admired companies (in the *Fortune* studies) are quoted in the major business press far more often than CEOs of less admired companies.

Examples of CEOs who have "taken up" an important new cause are Ross Perot's stand on public education in Texas and T. Boone Pickens' stand on shareholders rights (Sauerhaft and Atkins, 1989: 57). The point is that the stand must feature some new innovative ideas and it should in some way harmonize with the business of the company. Taking a stand for an important cause enhances the popular vision of the CEO and hence earns good will for the company's products. For example, care of the elderly might be a good topic for a pharmaceutical firm or child care might harmonize with a baby food firm. Very often dairies establish crusades to find "lost children" and circulate pictures of these children.

The second thing the firm might do is to contribute financially to causes. Here too, the cause should harmonize with the business. One large gift may have more impact than many small gifts. A contribution in the local area, for example to a city museum, may be much more visible to employees and consumers than a contribution to a large national museum like the Smithsonian Institute. We refer again to Richard Haayen's strategy at Allstate mentioned in Chapter 6. Here employees were encouraged to work as a group for local charities.

Sponsorship is another way to develop good will. A sports equipment firm may want to sponsor a sports event. If your product is sold to low-income groups, contribution to a baseball game may be preferable to sponsorship of a polo match. A sponsor is much more visible than a contributor so sponsorship of even a minor event may offer more "bang for the buck" than a simple contribution. Finally, Atkins and Sauerhaft point out that combining taking a stand, financial support, and sponsorship provides a very effective way to enhance the view of the firm and its products. It also provides much free publicity. The Ronald McDonald Houses provide a needed place for parents of hospitalized children to reside when they are visiting their children. Since children are big consumer of fast food, this is an ideal strategy. Being the only sponsor of this endeavor allows for a tremendous amount of PR and a large return on investment.

ESTABLISHING A GLOBAL IDENTITY

In the 1990s globalization has become a very important issue in business. The American Association of Collegiate Schools of Business (AACSB) has suggested that global emphasis should be an important component of business education. In our survey, both the CEOs and public relations specialists ranked globalization as a key issue for the 1990s. The experts warn that while globalization is a hot strategy for the 1990s, it is one that should be approached with caution.

Names, logos, and slogans for global marketing need careful analysis and development. Frank Delano, chair of Delano Goldman & Young, a New York-based consultant on corporate and brand identities, indicates that although there are tremendous opportunities for global marketing, creating the proper image abroad can be tricky. According to Katherine Burton (1990: 35), "What's out for the new decade are dehumanizing names and meaningless initials. What's in are names that suggest friendship and openness, and that can be easily translated into other languages." Burton also indicates that a company can avoid embarrassing situations by analyzing what its product or company name means in other languages. She cites the example, provided by Delano, of NYNEX, the New York telecommunications company. Its name sounds like the German word *nein*, which means no. This company might have trouble marketing its products in Germany. Also, according to Burton, Chesebrough-Ponds Inc. might find its Rave hair products getting some confused looks in Scandinavian countries; there its name denotes drunkenness."

To deal with the challenges involved in doing business with numerous other cultures, some companies employ people to deal only with protocol issues. Paul Burnham Finney (1990) indicates that protocol specialists are employed by companies such as United Technologies, AT&T, Boeing, and the Chase Manhattan Bank. According to Finney (p. 46), "Many of these masters of the Japanese tea ceremony, the hierarchy of British titles and the intricacies of the French plan de table are now expanding their spheres to include Eastern Europe." Learning and following protocol can be time-consuming and expensive, but it is an important factor in doing business worldwide. As Finney indicates, the protocol position does not necessarily have to be formalized; he (p. 49) quotes Letita Baldrige as saying that many polished executive secretaries often function as protocol officers, although they do not have the title. This is a good example of people being allowed to stretch their capabilities and perform in a way that is good for themselves as well as the firm.

This challenge of international marketing was brought home recently when Procter & Gamble attempted to globally market "Pert Plus," its combination shampoo-conditioner. As reported by Alecia Swasy (1990: B1), "The Pert Plus name couldn't be used in all markets. In some countries, similar-sounding names already were used for other products or it violated trademarks." According to Swasy, Procter & Gamble responded by dropping its usual practice of using one name for a product everywhere. To executives, that strategy was not as important as getting the shampoo-conditioner formula distributed as fast and as far as possible. This example shows that the challenges of international marketing go far beyond coping with a few cultural differences and legal restrictions.

CONVEYING IDENTITY IN THE MEDIA

Once a company has determined who they are and they have arranged opportunities for visibility, they have a new challenge. They now are faced with the media and other vehicles to convey their message. It is essential that, regardless of the vehicle used, the message be consistent. Public relations practitioners provide at least 40 percent of the daily content of the media and thus play an integral part of the nation's public information system (Cutlip, Center, and Broom 1985: 118).

Cutlip, Center, and Broom (1985) offer practitioners and CEOs a few basic principles for dealing with the media:

1. Shoot squarely
2. Give service
3. Do not beg or carp
4. Do not ask for kills (do not ask the media to stop a story)

5. Do not flood the media
6. Keep updated media lists

In his book, *Managing the Corporate Image*, James Gray, Jr., suggests that companies establish a corporate media or communications office. The office would be responsible for all media relationships. To accomplish this it must appoint a corporate spokesperson or spokespersons who will keep abreast of corporate policy and events. These spokespersons should establish sound contacts with the media, arranging for news conferences and briefings. They should disseminate news releases, and coach corporate spokespersons (and CEOs) in media relations and ways to handle interviews and conflict situations. This singular department can also ensure that the same overall message is conveyed internally and externally.

In our survey, the PR specialists point out the importance of media in determining corporate reputation and emphasize the media as an effective vehicle for reaching a variety of audiences with a single message. The CEOs, on the other hand, did not rely as heavily on the media for input but still felt it was essential to convey a consistent message.

While many companies have tried time and time again, they are faced with the reality that they cannot be everything to everyone. It is important for companies to know where they can make a difference. In other words, you should know your comparative advantage and milk it. Know and accept your limitations. Bjorn Borg, the tennis star, resisted the advice that many onlookers gave him, from the age of twelve on, to change his game. He insisted that, "It is important to find your own personality in the game, your own style. You have to find it, no one else can define it for you" (Safire and Safir 1990: 367). In some ways, it is the same with a corporation. Finding its own identity, being comfortable with itself, choosing its own style and personality are absolutely essential. People react favorably to individuality and confidence. Too many companies let themselves be done over by an outsider and find themselves playing a part that they

are not at all comfortable or familiar with. This does not bode
well for reputation.

EVALUATING IDENTITY AND
IMAGE PRESENTATION

Know your strengths and take advantage of them. Maybe you
can think of unique and profitable ways to market a perfectly
ordinary product. If you are mediocre in some things but superior
in others, think of every way possible to get the most from the
area you are superior in. This is similar to successful investors
in the stock market, who know where they have excellent, rather
than mediocre, skills. The process of establishing and maintaining
corporate reputation is an ongoing part of a management plan. In
our survey both the PR specialists and CEOs ranked evaluation
and re-evaluation as very important parts of the process. There
are a variety of ways which this can be accomplished.

One method to do this is to commission a study of what
your audiences have heard and what it means to them. Have
the study done by an objective party—perhaps an academic or
a professional survey firm. This study should not be undertaken
by your PR department, your marketing department, or your PR
consultants because they have a vested interest in seeing that their
work is well received.

Another way to examine the impact of your efforts would be
to explore the media coverage of your firm. A content analysis
of the favorability of the mentions of your company would pick
up the feelings of the media.

A study of the analyses of your company by such firms as
Value Line or the newsletters of the stock brokerage houses might
reveal the current state of your image in the financial world.

You might, as Peter Drucker (1990) recommends, take a leaf
from the book of Alfred P. Sloan, who built General Motors into
the world's premier manufacturing company in the 1920s and
1930s by working with customers. Once every three months he
would go to several dealerships in cities all over the United States.

Here he would work for several days as a salesman or assistant service manager. When he returned he would have new ideas on changing customer behavior, customer preferences, market style and trend, dealer service, and company service to dealers. Sloan spotted many more trends than did his expensive customer research departments. Similarly, the late Karl Bays, who made American Hospital Corporation a leader in its industry in the 1990s, would work as a salesperson for a two-week period twice a year. Other CEOs have gone out and watched what went on in their competitors' stores. They were able to spot many new trends like the importance of the two-worker family and the senior citizen markets. So Drucker advises the managers to walk around outside of their organizations (he assumes there is a good communications structure within the firm) and find out what is going on. Executives of each company should walk around in the markets and find out what customers, workers, financial analysts, media, environmentalists, and local and national government officials feel about their companies. This is the true test of success in building your company's good reputation.

CHAPTER 10

Improving Corporate Reputation
Now and in the Future:
A Checklist

So many skills come together to form a good reputation. The company desperately needs a CEO at the top who is capable of organizing the firm in such a way that people really work together. Companies need an environment that recognizes the unique skills of each person and uses those skills to form a united whole. It all comes back to good management. It is no fluke that the evaluators in the *Fortune* survey consistently rate quality of management at the top of the list of eight determinants of a good reputation.

What causes good reputation and what follows from good reputation is circular. Look at the eight determinants of good reputation according to *Fortune*. Innovativeness, for example, can create a good reputation; but having a good reputation may enable the firm to be more innovative. This is true of all eight determinants.

According to Opinion Research Corporation's 1987 study, seven Americans in ten (70 percent) feel that a company's reputation depends more on what the company itself does than on events outside the company and beyond its control (1988). Although it is possible that good corporate reputation can arise from factors such as responsible behavior on the part of top executives and all employees, excellent products, good service, good treatment of workers and of the surrounding community, it would seem that many well-meaning companies fail to meet their expectations because they have not carefully planned their relationship with the audiences they intend to reach. There are many approaches a company can take to improve its corporate reputation. This chapter summarizes in checklist form ideas for improving reputation and outlines proactive measures that a firm can take to boost its reputation. (These ideas are presented in depth in chapters 6 through 9.)

The corporation interacts with a variety of constituencies in many ways. The audience matrix as presented by Stan Sauerhaft and Chris Atkins (1989) includes such groups as company management, employees, unions, suppliers, customers, financial and investment companies, the local community, and local, state, and federal officials. These constituents react to a wide range of events in the life of the corporation such as a new CEO, a new product introduction, layoffs, corporate crime, corporate philanthropy, quarterly and annual reports, environmental issues, and the relocation of an office or plant.

In dealing with constituencies as defined above, firms are advised by Sauerhaft and Atkins to assess relationships by talking to people and by using surveys. Second, they can put themselves in the place of each constituent and see what they would expect and want. The companies are further advised to develop a matrix where the columns are the constituencies (such as government, customers, and employees) and the rows are the company actions that affect them (i.e., product change, change in CEO). Once the columns and rows are set, the company should focus on proper policies and action steps with respect to each constituency and action.

We might say that the best way to acquire a good reputation is to deserve it! Thus, the best advice might be: "Don't learn the tricks of the trade. Learn the trade" (anonymous, cited in Safire and Safir 1990: 15). But deserving a good reputation and actually having one may be two different things. Therefore, in discussing ways to improve corporate reputation, one must necessarily cover two aspects of the topic: deserving a good reputation and convincing others that this is the case.

WAYS TO ATTRACT AND KEEP QUALITY WORKERS (CHAPTER 6)

1. Encourage worker creativity in many areas.
   a. Produce creative annual reports.
   b. Foster and facilitate employee community service.
   c. Develop unique ways of motivating and rewarding employees for creativity.
   d. Lead the pack with new products.
   e. Brainstorm on a regular basis to generate and foster the development of new ideas, not only for advertising and public relations but for work at all levels.
2. Empower employees to provide good service.
3. Motivate workers.
4. Force yourself to keep the long term in view.
5. Develop personnel policies that stress longevity.

As total quality management has become a key slogan for American industry, we briefly review ways to assure consumer satisfaction with the quality of products.

WAYS TO BUILD A REPUTATION FOR QUALITY OF PRODUCTS AND SERVICES (CHAPTER 7)

1. Emphasize quality service and tell the public about it.
2. Make it company policy to apologize for poor service.

3. Determine customer requirements and expectations.

4. Carefully manage customer relationships.

5. Set customer service standards.

6. Stress commitment to customers.

7. Have a plan for complaint resolution.

8. Develop methods of determining consumer satisfaction.

9. Assess consumer satisfaction results.

10. Compare consumer satisfaction ratings with those of competitors.

As firms must be and appear to be financially sound to continue their lives, we review some ways to cultivate a reputation for financial soundness.

WAYS TO IMPROVE FINANCIAL SOUNDNESS AND CORPORATE REPUTATION (CHAPTER 8)

1. Research your company, your policies, and your competitors' activities before you hire public relations consultants or change your name, logo, or policies.

2. Cultivate good relationships with shareholders.

3. Even in bad times, keep your company reputation in the public eye.

4. Respond to bad news immediately and confidently.

5. Develop a crisis control center.

Finally, we will look at how to ascertain, establish, and publicize corporate identity.

USING PUBLIC RELATIONS TO IDENTIFY AND ESTABLISH CORPORATE IDENTITY (CHAPTER 9)

1. Have a program to establish and constantly re-evaluate your identity.

2. Persuade people to recognize the value of your product and who you are.
3. Take action to increase visibility in domestic markets.
4. Take action to increase visibility in global markets.
5. Take steps to convey your identity to the media.
6. Constantly re-evaluate your identity and image presentation.

We have examined current research studies, popular descriptions, and measurements of corporate reputation. From these studies we have distilled ideas for the improvement of reputation. As a final caution we must be aware that times change and the determinants of corporate reputation change too. For example, "corporate governance" seems to be an important investor demand emerging in the 1990s. Up to now, the *Fortune* surveys have not dealt specifically with this. It is really important for firms to keep up with current and emerging determinants of corporate reputation. You cannot earn a good reputation now and in the future by meeting demands that have become outdated!

References

Ackerman, Lawrence D. "Identity Strategies That Make a Difference." *Journal of Business Strategy* (May/June 1988): 28–32.

Alexander, Gordon J., and Rogene A. Bucholtz. "Corporate Social Responsibility and Stockmarket Performance." *Academy of Management Journal* 21 (1978): 479–486.

Alpert, Mark. "Should You Invest in a Long-Term CEO?" *Fortune* (July 2, 1990): 10.

Aupperle, Kenneth E., Archie B. Carroll, and John D. Hatfield. "An Empirical Examination of the Relationship Between Corporate Social Responsibility and Profitability." *Academy of Management Journal* 28 (1985): 446–463.

Baig, Edward C. "America's Most Admired Corporations." *Fortune* (January 19, 1987): 18–30.

Balachandra, R. "Winning the Race to the Marketplace." *Wall Street Journal*, April 30, 1990, p. A14.

Band, William A. "Build Your Company Image to Increase Sales." *Sales and Marketing Management in Canada* (Canada) 23/11 (December 1987): 10–11.

Beales, H., Craswell, R. and Salop, S. "Information Remedies for

Consumer Protection." *American Economic Review* 71 (May 1981): 410–413.

Bennett, Amanda. "For Chief Executives, Knowing When to Leave Post May Be Toughest Decision." *Wall Street Journal*, June 8, 1990, pp. B1, B3.

————. "Making the Grade with the Customer." *Wall Street Journal*, November 12, 1990, pp. B1, B4.

————. "Many Consumers Expect Better Service—And Say They Are Willing to Pay for It." *Wall Street Journal*, November 12, 1990, p. B1.

————. "When Money Is Tight, Bosses Scramble for Other Ways to Motivate the Troops." *Wall Street Journal*, October 31, 1990, pp. B1, B5.

Berg, Eric, N. "How Much Should Companies Tell?" *New York Times*, July 17, 1990, pp. D1, D8.

Bernstein, Leopold A., and Joel G. Siegel. "The Concept of Earnings Quality," *Financial Analysts Journal* 35/4 (July/August 1979): 72–75.

Blume, Marshall E. "On the Assessment of Risk." *Journal of Finance* (March 1971): 1–10.

Bosch, Jean-Claude, and Mark Hirschey. "The Valuation Effects of Corporate Name Changes." *Financial Management* (Winter 1989).

Bowman, Edward H., and Mason Haire. "A Strategic Posture Towards CSR." *California Management Review* 18/2 (1975): 49–58.

Brouillard, Joseph. "Corporate Reputation Counts." *Advertising Age* 54/48 (November 14, 1983): M-46.

Brouillette, Geoff. "The CEO's Role in P.R." *United States Banker* 98/8 (August 1987): 36–40.

Brown, Paul B., and Martha E. Mangelsdorf. "Tex's Chain Saw Manicure." *Inc.* 9/12 (November 1987): 130–134.

Budd, John F., Jr. "Wanted: A Corporate Champion." *Wall Street Journal*, April 16, 1990, p. A12.

Burton, Katherine. "Bucks in a Name." *Daily News* (Business Section), March 5, 1990, p. 35.

Carr, Clay. *Front–Line Customer Service*. Wiley, 1990.

"Centenial Journal: 100 Years in Business—Chicago's Poisoned Tylenol Scare, 1982." *Wall Street Journal*, November 29, 1989, p. B1.

Chajet, Cline, "The Making of a New Corporate Image." *Journal of Business Strategy* (May/June 1989): 18–20.

"Corporate Eyes, Ears and Mouths." *Economist* (March 18, 1989): 67–68.

Crossen, Cynthia. "Simple Apology for Poor Service Is in Sorry State." *Wall Street Journal*, November 29, 1990, p. B1.

Crovitz, Clive. "The Making of a New Corporate Image. *Journal of Business Strategy* (May/June 1989): 18–20.

Cutlip, Scott M., Allen H. Center, and Glen M. Broom. *Effective Public Relations*. Prentice–Hall, 1985.

Davenport, Carol. "America's Most Admired Corporations." *Fortune* (January 30, 1989): 68–94.

DeCarlo, Neil J., and W. Kent Sterett. "History of the Malcolm Baldrige National Quality Award." *Quality Progress* (March 1990): 21–27.

DeJong, Douglas V., Robert Forsythe, and Russell J. Lundholm. "Ripoffs, Lemons, and Reputation Formation in Agency Relationships: A Laboratory Market Study." *Journal of Finance* 40 (July 1985): 809–820.

Devaney, Mike. "Risk, Commitment, and Project Abandonment." *Journal of Business Ethics* 10/2 (February 1991): 157–159.

Diamond, Douglas W. "Reputation Acquisition in Debt Markets." *Journal of Political Economy* 97/4 (1989): 828–862.

Diffenbach, John, and Richard B. Higgins. "Strategic Credibility Can Make a Difference." *Business Horizons* 30 (May/June 1987): 13–18.

Dobson, John. "Corporate Reputation: A Free–Market Solution to Unethical Behavior." *Business & Society* 28/1 (Spring 1989): 1–5.

Dorfman, John R. "As Debt Becomes a Dirty Word, Low-Leveraged Firms Win Fans." *Wall Street Journal*, January 31, 1991, pp. C1–C2.

Drucker, Peter, "Manage by Walking Around—Outside." *Wall Street Journal*, May 11, 1990, p. A12.

———. "The Discipline of Innovation," *Harvard Business Review* (May/June 1985): 67–72.

Faber, David. "Investor Relations, Pfizer's Costly Delay." *Institutional Investor* (June 1990): 189.

Falvey, Rodney, E. "Trade, Quality Reputations and Commercial Policy," *International Economic Review* 30/3 (August 1989): 60–62.

Feucht, Frederic N. "It's Symbolic: Is Your Corporate Logo Sending the Right Message to the Right People?" *American Demographics* 11/11 (November 1989): 30–33.

Finney, Paul Burnham. "Global Deals: The Faux Pas Factor." *New York Times Magazine*, June 10, 1990.

Fischer, Anne B. "Spiffing Up the Corporate Image." *Fortune* 114/2 (July 21, 1986): 68–72.

———. "Glamour: Getting It—Or Getting It Back." *Fortune* 113/20 (May 12, 1986): 18–22.

Fischer, Howard M. "Wanted: Director for Troubled Company." *Directors and Boards* 13/1 (Fall 1988): 23–26.

Freedman, Alix M. "Most Consumers Shun Luxuries, Seek Few Frills but Better Service." *Wall Street Journal*, September 19, 1989, pp. B1–B4.

Friedman, Stewart D. "Succession Systems in Large Corporations: Characteristics and Correlates of Performance." *Human Resource Management* 25 (Summer 1986): 191–213.

Frohman, Mark, and Perry Pascarella. "How to Write a Purpose Statement." *Industry Week* 232 (March 23, 1987): 31–34.

Fuchsberg, Gilbert. "Gurus of Quality Are Gaining Clout." *Wall Street Journal*, November 27, 1990, pp. B1–B7.

———. "Let Restraint Guide Your Advertising, Baldrige Prize Winners to be Warned." *Wall Street Journal*, January 11, 1991, p. B5.

———. "Nonprofits May Get Own Baldrige Prizes." *Wall Street Journal*, March 14, 1991, p. B1.

Galant, Debbie. "Gimmicks of the Year." *Institutional Investor* (April 1990): 124–126.

Garbett, Thomas. *How To Build a Corporation's Identity and Project Its Image.* Lexington Books, 1988.

Girifalco, Louis A. "The Dynamics of Technological Change." *Wharton Magazine* 7/1 (Fall 1982): 31–37.

Gladstone, William L., and Ray J. Groves. "Ernst & Young Scotches a Rumor." *Wall Street Journal*, December 11, 1990, p. A19.

"Good Corporate Reputation Boosts Sales." *Christian Science Monitor* 81 (April 24, 1989): 9.

Gottschalk, Earl C., Jr. "Staying Local Can Be Smart for Investors." *Wall Street Journal*, May 16, 1990, pp. C1, C2.

Gray, James G., Jr. *Managing the Corporate Image*. Quorum, 1986.

Grenig, James E., and Todd Hunt. *Managing Public Relations*. Holt, Rinehart and Winston, 1984.

Gurnee, Robert F. "Ethical Value and Business Leadership." *Review of Business* 10/3 (Winter 1988): 4–6.

Hartigan, Maureen F. "Organizing for Global Identity." *Journal of Business & Industrial Marketing* 2/3 (Summer 1987): 65–73.

"How a CEO Expresses His Devotion to Quality." *Wall Street Journal*, April 20, 1990, p. B1.

"How a Corporation Reveals Itself." *New York Times Forum*, October 14, 1990, p. F13.

"How CU Tests and Rates Cars." *Consumer Reports* (April 1991): 250–255.

Howard, Robert. "Values Make the Company: An Interview with Robert Hass," *Harvard Business Review* (September/October 1990): 133–144.

Hutton, Cynthia. "America's Most Admired Corporations." *Fortune* (January 6, 1986): 16–27.

"Is Detroit Closing the Reliability Gap." *Consumer Reports* (April 1991): 248–249.

Kanner, Bernice. "A McDitty for the Nineties." *New York* (June 18, 1990): 16.

Kanter, Rosabeth Moss. "Championing Change: An Interview with Bell Atlantic's CEO Raymond Smith." *Harvard Business Review* (January/February 1991): 119–130.

King, Thomas R. "Credibility Gap: More Consumers Find Celebrity Ads Unpersuasive." *Wall Street Journal*, July 5, 1989, p. B5.

———. "Philip Morris Smoke to Shed Yuppie Image." *Wall Street Journal*, February 2, 1990, p. B1.

Knowles, Anne. "An Electronics Company by Any Other Name." *Electronic Business* 15/6 (March 20, 1989): 54–55.

Kreps, David M., and R. Wilson. "Reputation and Imperfect Information." *Journal of Economic Theory* 27 (August 1982): 235–279.

Kunde, Diana. "In the Driver's Seat: Automakers Shifting to Service Emphases." *Dallas Morning News*, March 24, 1991, pp. 1H, 10H, 11H.

Kydd, Christine T., John R. Ogilvie, and L. Allen Slade. "I Don't Care What They Say, as Long as They Spell My Name Right:

Publicity,ReputationandTurnover."*Group&OrganizationStudies* 15/1 (March 1990): 53–74.

Leonard, Maria. "Challenges to the Termination-at-Will Doctrine." *Personnel Administrator* 28 (1983): 49–56.

McConnell, Nancy Belliveau. "Winning on the Slow Track." *Institutional Investor* (October 1988): 195–208.

McGuire, Jean B., Alison Sundgren, and Thomas Schneeweis. "Corporate Social Responsibility and Firm Financial Performance." *Academy of Management Journal* 31/4 (1988): 854–872.

Makin, Claire. "Ranking Corporate Reputations." *Fortune* 107/1 (January 10, 1983): 34–44.

Margulies, Walter P. "Corporate Image and the P/E Ratio: They Often Go Hand in Hand." *Management Review* 68/10 (October 1979): 16–19.

Mason, Richard D. "The Office of the Future as a Socio-Technical System." *Infotech State of the Art Report*, 1980 Series 3, pp. 140–150.

Meyers, William. *The Image-Makers: Power and Persuasion on Madison Avenue.* New York Times Books, 1984.

Milgrom, Paul, and John Roberts. "Predation, Reputation, and Entry Deterrence." *Journal of Economic Theory* 27 (August 1982): 280–312.

Miller, Richard B. "Why Some Banks Can't Tell the Truth." *Banker's Monthly* 104/2 (February 1987) 13–15.

Miller, William H. "Sprucing Up the Corporate Image." *Industry Week* 214 (August 23, 1982): 35–41.

Moody's Handbook of Common Stock. Moody's Investors Service, 1982.

Moskal, Brian S. "Can Audi Make It Bank?" *Industry Week* 236/3 (February 1, 1988): 49–50.

Moskowitz, M. "Choosing Socially Responsible Stocks." *Business and Society* 1 (1972): 71–75.

Nie, Norman H., et al. *Statistical Package for the Social Sciences.* 2d ed. McGraw–Hill, 1975.

Nolan, Joseph. "To Gain a Good Reputation." *Bell Atlantic Quarterly* (Summer 1985).

Olins, Wally. "Corporate Identity." *Economist* 109/1 (January 6, 1990): 50–62.

———. "How a Corporation Reveals Itself." *New York Times Forum*, October 14, 1990, p. F13.

Parket, J. Robert, and Henry Eilbirt. "Social Responsibility: The Underlying Factors." *Business Horizons* 18 (1975): 5–10.

Pearson, Andrall E. "Tough Minded Ways to Get Innovative." *Harvard Business Review* (May/June 1988): 99.

Perry, Nancy J. "America's Most Admired Corporations." *Fortune* 109/1 (January 9, 1984): 50–62.

Picker, Ida. "Do CFOs Really Make Good CEOs?" *Institutional Investor* (August 1989): 47–50.

Pollock, Ellen Joan. "Lawyers Abandon Resistance to PR Firms." *Wall Street Journal*, March 14, 1990, pp. B1, B5.

"Public Relations, Store Tie-Ins Launch 'Green' Cosmetics Line." *Public Relations Journal* (April 1991): 24–25.

Putka, Gary. "Business, Colleges Can Teach Each Other: An Interview with Richard Cyert." *Wall Street Journal*, April 13, 1990, p. B1.

Rappaport, Alfred. "Let's Let Business Be Business." *New York Times Forum*, February 4, 1990, p. F13.

Rawl, Lawrence. "Exxon Strikes Back." *Time* (March 25, 1990): 62–63.

Rigdon, Joan E. "More Firms Try to Reward Good Service, but Incentives May Backfire in Long Run." *Wall Street Journal*, December 5, 1990, pp. B1, B6.

Robert, Michel M. "Managing Your Competitor's Strategy." *Journal of Business Strategy* (March/April 1990): 24–28.

————. *The Strategist CEO: How Visionary Executives Build Organizations*. Quorum, 1989.

Rogerson, William P. "Reputation and Product Quality." *Bell Journal of Economics* 14/2 (Autumn 1983): 508–516.

Rosecranz, Richard. "Too Many Bosses, Too Few Workers." *New York Times Forum*, July 15, 1990, p. F11.

Safire, William, and Leonard Safir (eds.). *Words of Wisdom: More Good Advice*. Simon & Schuster, 1990.

Sauerhaft, Stan, and Chris Atkins. *Image Wars: Protecting Your Company When There's No Place to Hide*. Wiley, 1989.

Schultz, Ellen. "America's Most Admired Corporations." *Fortune* 117/2 (January 18, 1988): 32–37.

Schultz, Ray. "Satisfaction Guaranteed for Customers and Crew." *Wall Street Journal*, January 28, 1991, p. A10.

Schwadel, Francine. "Lands' End Stumbles as Fashion Shifts Away from Retailer's Traditional Fare." *Wall Street Journal*, April 27, 1990, pp. B1, B2.

Schwoerer, Catherine, and Benson Rosen. "Effects of Employment-at-Will Policies and Compensation Policies on Corporate Image and Job Pursuit Intentions." *Journal of Applied Psychology* 74/4 (1989): 653–656.

Selame, Elinor, and Joe Selame. *The Company Image: Building Your Identity and Influence in the Marketplace.* Wiley, 1988.

Sellers, Patricia. "America's Most Admired Corporations." *Fortune* 111/1 (January 7, 1985): 18–30.

Serafin, Raymond, "W.B. Doner Hits a Gusher." *Advertising Age* 59/24 (June 6, 1988): 43.

Shapiro, Carl. "Consumer Information, Product Quality and Seller Reputation." *Bell Journal of Economics* 13 (1982): 20–35.

———. "Premiums for High Quality Products as Returns to Reputations." *Quarterly Journal of Economics* (November 1983): 659–679.

Siconolfi, Michael. "Merrill Revamps Brokers' Training, Pay." *Wall Street Journal*, December 11, 1990, p. C1.

Sinkula, James M., and Leanne Lawtor. "Bank Characteristics and Consumer Bank Choice: How Important Are Importance Measures." *Journal of Professional Services Marketing* 3/3–4 (1988): 131–141.

Smith, Craig. "Philanthropy as a Business Tactic." *New York Times Forum*, December 30, 1990, p. F11.

Smith, Donald G. "Why Does He Keep Those Cups and Saucers Flying?" *Wall Street Journal*, August 28, 1989, p. A8.

Smith, Patrick J. "How to Present Your Firm to the World." *Journal of Business Strategy* (January/February 1990): 32–36.

Smith, Sarah. "America's Most Admired Corporations." *Fortune* 21/3 (January 29, 1990): 58–92.

Sobol, Marion G., and Gail Farrelly. "Corporate Reputation: A Function of Relative Size or Financial Performance." *Review of Business and Economic Research* (Fall 1988): 45–59.

Soloman, R., and K. Hansen. *It's Good Business.* Atheneum, 1985.

Sponseller, Diane. "Goodwill: A Tangible or Intangible Ratemaking Component?" *Public Utilities Fortnightly* 124/4 (August 17, 1989): 43–47.

Sprout, Alison L. "America's Most Admired Corporations." *Fortune* (February 11, 1991): 52–82.

Subramanian, Sethuraman. "Motivation by Fear Can't Improve Quality." *Wall Street Journal,* April 13, 1990, p. A11.

Swasy, Alecia. "How Innovation at P&G Restored Luster to Washed-Up Pert and Made It No. 1." *Wall Street Journal,* December 6, 1990, p. B1.

Taylor, William. "The Business of Innovation." *Harvard Business Review* 68/2 (March/April 1990): 87–106.

Thackray, John. "America's Corporate Hype." *Management Today* (March 1987): 68–75.

"The Best and the Brightest." *Institutional Investor* (August 1989): 58–69.

Tomsho, Robert. "Wal-Mart's Walton Predicts Company Could Quintuple Sales by the Year 2000." *Wall Street Journal,* June 4, 1990, p. B9.

Tsui, Anne S. "A Role Set Analysis of Managerial Reputation." *Organizational Behavior and Human Performance* 34 (1984): 64–96.

Ullmann, A. "Data in Search of a Theory: A Critical Examination of the Relationship among Social Performance, Social Disclosure and Economic Performance." *Academy of Management Review* 10 (1985): 540–577.

U. S. Department of Commerce. *Application Guidelines* for the Malcolm Baldrige National Quality Award, 1991.

"USA's 1991 Shareholder 1000." *United Shareholders Association Advocate* 6/4 (April 1991): 3–6.

Vance, Stanley C. "Are Socially Responsible Firms Good Investment Risks?" *Management Review* 64 (1975): 18–24.

Verity, John W. "Upstarts Outshine the Stars." *Datamation* 30/19 (November 15, 1984): 34–52.

Waldholz, Michael. "Merck to Cut Some Prices for California." *Wall Street Journal,* June 19, 1990, p. B4.

Wayne, Leslie. "Board Shifts Called Manipulative." *New York Times,* March 18, 1991, p. D2.

Webber, Alan M. "Consensus, Continuity, and Common Sense: An Interview with Compaq's Rod Canion." *Harvard Business Review* (July/August 1990): 115–123.

Weigelt, Keith, and Colin Camerer. "Reputation and Corporate Strategy: A Review of Recent Theory and Applications." *Strategic Management Journal* 9 (1988): 443–454.

Weiner, Steve. "Do They Speak Spanish in Kansas City?" *Forbes* 141/2 (January 25, 1988): 46–47.

Welch, John F., Jr. "We've Got to Simplify and Delegate More." (March 26, 1990): 30–158.

"What's in a Name." *Fortune* 116 (September 14, 1987): 6.

White, James A. "Grassroots Research Sometimes Catches Analysts Off Balance." *Wall Street Journal*, May 1, 1990, pp. C1, C27.

———. "Shareholder-Rights Movement Sways a Number of Big Companies." *Wall Street Journal*, April 4, 1991, pp. C1, C16.

White, Joseph B. "GM's Plan to Boost Pensions Criticized: Executives Regret Making Issue Public." *Wall Street Journal*, May 29, 1990, p.A3.

Williams, Kerstin. "Boosting Publicity Through Research: 16 Keys to Profitable PR." *Business Marketing* 70/10 (October 1985): 124–129.

Winslow, Ron. "Merck Plans Medicaid Price Cut." *Wall Street Journal*, April 23, 1990, pp. B1, B4.

Wisenblit, Joseph Z. "Person Positioning: Empirical Evidence and a Paradigm." *Journal of Professional Services Marketing* 4/2 (1989): 51–82.

Index

About the Authors

MARION G. SOBOL is Professor of Management Information Science at the Edwin L. Cox School of Business at Southern Methodist University. Her research focuses on labor force, economic performance, computerization, statistics, and quality issues. She is co-author of three books and publishes regularly in such journals as *Information and Management, Review of Economics and Statistics, Social Science Quarterly, Journal of Human Resources*, and *Review of Business and Economic Research*.

GAIL E. FARRELLY is Associate Professor of Accounting at Rutgers University. Her research focuses on financial reporting issues and on the perception, analysis, and disclosure of investment risk. An expert in behavioral finance, she has served as a Visiting Scholar at Batterymatch Financial Management, where she did research on the risk tolerance of institutional investors. She has published in such journals as *The Accounting Review, Financial Analysts Journal, Financial Management*, and *The Journal of Portfolio Management*.

JESSICA S. TAPER is a public relations specialist in Dallas, Texas. She has worked for a noted international public relations agency, an advertising firm, a university public information office, a municipal agency, and a national public accounting firm. She is a graduate of the University of Texas with a Bachelor of Journalism degree in the Public Relations sequence.

DATE DUE

~~AUG 1 6 1994~~	~~JAN 0 7 1998~~
~~FEB 1 7 1997~~	~~FEB 1 7 1998~~
~~OC~~	~~MAY 1~~
~~NOV 2 8 1997~~	~~2008~~
~~MAR 3 1 1998~~	
~~JAN 0 6 195~~ ~~2008~~	
~~NOV 0 7 2000~~	
~~MAY 1 6 2001~~	